THINKING
DIAGRAMS

THINKING DIAGRAMS

PROCESSING AND CONNECTING EXPERIENCES, FACTS, AND IDEAS

Mickey Kolis and Benjamin H. Kolis

ROWMAN & LITTLEFIELD
Lanham • Boulder • New York • London

Published by Rowman & Littlefield
A wholly owned subsidiary of The Rowman & Littlefield Publishing Group, Inc.
4501 Forbes Boulevard, Suite 200, Lanham, Maryland 20706
www.rowman.com

Unit A, Whitacre Mews, 26-34 Stannary Street, London SE11 4AB,
United Kingdom

British Library Cataloguing in Publication Information Available

Library of Congress Cataloging-in-Publication Data

Names: Kolis, Mickey, 1954– author. | Kolis, Benjamin H., author.
Title: Thinking diagrams : processing and connecting experiences, facts, and
 ideas / Mickey Kolis and Benjamin H. Kolis.
Description: Lanham, Maryland : Rowman & Littlefield, 2016. | Includes
 bibliographical references.
Identifiers: LCCN 2016013459 (print) | LCCN 2016025323 (ebook) | ISBN
 9781475828672 (cloth : alk. paper) | ISBN 9781475828689 (pbk.) | ISBN
 9781475828696 (electronic)
Subjects: LCSH: Thought and thinking—Study and teaching. | Critical
 thinking—Study and teaching. | Metacognition.
Classification: LCC LB1590.3 .K6554 2016 (print) | LCC LB1590.3 (ebook) | DDC
 370.15/22—dc23
LC record available at https://lccn.loc.gov/2016013459

∞™ The paper used in this publication meets the minimum requirements
of American National Standard for Information Sciences—Permanence of
Paper for Printed Library Materials, ANSI/NISO Z39.48-1992.

Printed in the United States of America

CONTENTS

ACKNOWLEDGMENTS

BEN'S STORY

Thinking Diagrams has been an exhilarating—and challenging—project.

I want to thank Henry MacCarthy and Rebecca Fremo, my mentors and friends, who model how good people, thinkers, and professionals behave. They have beauty in their hearts and it shows in their work.

Of course, thanks to Dad for taking me with him on this journey. His vision persisted through several fundamental changes and revisions (not to mention the years the diagrams spent crashing around in his head), and I was thrilled to contribute.

Thanks to Mom, whose patience and love is unending (I hope), and to my partner, Teige, who makes me think and forgive, and who makes really great salads.

MICKEY'S STORY

Thinking sure is hard work! Putting the diagrams together has been one of the most challenging tasks I have ever attempted.

Toward that end, I would like to thank my Montana State University-Northern colleagues whom I made listen to me think out loud while looking at all those beginning diagrams. When they started running away when they saw me, I feared I had gone too far! Such is life. I would also like to thank my MSU–N students who learned the diagrams with me in my Introduction to Brain-Compatible Learning class, added their own thoughts and perspectives and helped me get those diagrams into this final (for now) form.

Any book writing is a journey. I would like to thank my son Ben for being such an amazing collaborator. While the ideas are mostly mine, the vast majority of the words are his—and I like how they fall. Thank you, Ben, for all your time, effort, and work on this project.

A big-shout out also goes to Matthew Mitchell, who contributed all the diagrams you will see in the book. He was able to take my ideas and make them look presentable—no small feat!!

As always I would also like to give a shout-out to my wife, Jeanne—she is wonderful. Her support, insights, and listening skills help keep me focused on what really matters.

INTRODUCTION

I once took a graduate-level teaching class where we learned how to respond to students' answers: correct answers, partially correct answers, and just plain wrong answers. We learned how to use wait time, how to call on different students and how to ask "higher-order questions." Those were all good things to know and I have used most of those strategies from that point on in my classrooms.

The fact of the matter is that most teachers ask their students lots of questions—and most of those questions are fact based (content oriented). We ask content-based questions because we think it increases student learning and engagement; we want to see if they have read (and understood) the material; it is how we went through school; we know how to organize our teaching around that strategy; and isn't that what the Socratic Method is?

We've learned a lot about how the brain works since I took that class oh so many years ago. We know about the structures of the brain (right and left as well as front and back), multiple intelligences, the way that facts are stored, and cognitive belief systems. We also know about Bloom's Taxonomy, higher-order thinking skills and some developmental features of intellect.

And yet, it's still unclear how to teach students to "think" (*Merriam-Webster*, 2002), defined as "to use one's mind actively to form connected ideas." Content is king. We can see it in our tests (classroom and standardized), our grading, and the types of reading material we assign. Most schooling is fact based, and most teachers have little conceptual knowledge of what makes a higher-order thinking question more complex than a run-of-the-mill content-based question.

And most teachers feel it. They might question the relevance of all these facts: How important is it really to know that Helena is the capital of Montana? I mean really, in the grand scheme of things? Not knowing "why" is uncomfortable, sure, but what's the alternative? In many schools, there isn't one: Resources are limited, time is limited, and no one is getting paid for being a revolutionary.

The problem is, it's not clear and explicit what questions make students actually think for themselves. Furthermore, 1) it isn't clear *how* certain questions make students think, nor 2) *what type of thinking* is required of students to answer certain types of questions. Without some nuanced answers to these questions, it's just plain easier to teach content.

Easier, yes, but if the real focus of teaching is student "learning" (defined in *Merriam-Webster* [2002] as a "change in thoughts, beliefs or actions"), teaching for only content fact accumulation falls far short of our goal. We have to provide students the opportunities to practice "thinking," and do so in an environment where failure is not high stakes. We have to develop their habits of mind. This requires us to be Explicit and Intentional about student "thinking"!

Teaching thinking is also a relevance issue. Memorization by itself isn't relevant. We have access to more facts than we can handle with a click of a mouse or the swipe of an index finger. Memorizing facts doesn't improve your quality of life (in the long term anyway), but improving your ability to think, or being able to think in different ways does. My (Ben talking here) high school math teacher used to say, "Are you going to walk around on the street with a calculator in your pocket?" I wonder if he ever imagined that the answer would be a resounding, "YES!"

The reality of our present world is different than we imagined, and memorization is taking a backseat to processing and connecting information and ideas. Being able to think increases your chances of workable/success-oriented solutions. Making thinking the focus of classrooms allows students to replace their current patterns (of thought, belief, or actions) with patterns that may be more effective in meeting their needs.

This book is unique not because it identifies higher-order thinking skills, but because it models thinking using a progressively complex series of diagrams which make "thinking" Explicit. We can intentionally teach thinking because it is explicit (and therefore measurable). By making thinking explicit, we can teach certain types of thinking "Intentionally." These diagrams allow us to Plan, and Re-meditate, student misunderstandings when they occur, right then and there with a strategy grounded in success.

Learning is a hugely personal process. Teachers know they can't make anyone learn anything if the learner doesn't want to. But when we teach "thinking" explicitly, we empower our students to improve their lives and (a key point of this book) make ourselves dispensable.

This book is organized into five parts. Part I explains big-picture ideas: the Knowledge, Skills, and Dispositions of teaching Thinking Questions (TQ), as well as issues of relevance. Part I does not include any diagrams (just hold your horses). Part II introduces the simplest set of diagrams and focuses on experiences in general and their formation and structure. This is where thinking begins. Part III offers advanced higher-thinking skills which focus on illuminating past experiences. Part IV offers examples into how thinking looks with a future orientation. Part V talks about the complex issue of "planning for student learning" with the Thinking Questions in mind.

So imagine this book as a Master Teacher's Education Class. We will follow a teacher (Mr. James) and some of his students as they explore thinking and Thinking Questions (TQs). We will connect the Knowledge, Skills and Dispositions of teaching thinking—and then start at the beginning of how we come to know things. Creating the Art of Teaching Thinking is a journey—so grab that handrail and hold on for the ride!

I

WHY THINKING QUESTIONS?

Before we talk about teaching thinking, we should first think a little about what "thinking" is. *Merriam-Webster* (2002) says that thinking is "to believe that something is true, that a particular situation exists, that something will happen, etc." or "to have an opinion about something or to form or have a thought in your mind."

That's a solid place to start. That is, after all, what we hope to accomplish—we want students to form their own opinions, to have a broad worldview, to consider cause and effect, to have thoughts. But how do you teach that? How do you bridge the gap between presenting content and student thinking? Bloom's Taxonomy identifies some higher-order thinking skills:

- Knowledge/Remembering
- Comprehension/Understanding
- Application
- Analysis
- Evaluation
- Synthesis/Creating

These are the different "ways" to think, all of which are useful terms and a great place to start. But the problem isn't really knowing which higher-order thinking skills to teach: The question is *how*. How do you teach synthesis? Or analysis, or evaluation? How do you make "thinking" in those ways Explicit and Intentional?

For example, how do you "teach" students to Summarize (a comprehension question)? Or Interpret (an analysis question)? Or Categorize (a synthesis question)? Or even Judge (an evaluation question)? We can (and frequently do) ask these types of questions—but "teach" students to think in those ways? Not usually—mostly because we do not have a framework for understanding how the brain needs to work in order to answer those questions.

So with that in mind, why Thinking Questions (TQ)? We live in an information-rich environment where facts can be accessed/gathered almost instantaneously. Recalling or having access to the facts of a content area is different than understanding how to use them or how they work together to create understanding.

Knowing facts is not "thinking," just like listing the titles of the "100 Best Movies" does not make you a cinematographer. Thinking (rather than memorizing) requires that the learner DO something with the information. At the deepest level thinking connects what you know (knowledge) with what you can do (skills) to why you choose to do it (dispositions).

Ben's Story: Last summer I was asked to audition for a musical. At the audition, they asked how much singing experience I had (a little) and whether I could tap dance (not at all). But I'd played soccer for many years and I've always liked to learn new physical skills, so I learned a small section of a dance, laughed, had some fun, and left the audition thinking I'd probably be offered a small ensemble role. The next day I was offered the lead.

It turns out, what had impressed the choreographer wasn't my skill or knowledge, but my dispositions—my attitude.

Knowledge—how to tap dance—very little to none at all!

Skill—tap dancing itself—no!

Disposition—willingness to practice and learn the knowledge and skills— absolutely!!!

So what might knowledge, skills and dispositions look like in the classroom? Part I introduces Rachel, Ramone, Jack, and Sarah, and their American history teacher, Mr. James, who teaches using Thinking Questions.

It's the first day of a new American history class. Rachel, Ramone, Jack, and Sarah are sitting with their friends and classmates waiting for the first bell.

Rachel is a straight-A student with her eyes set on a top college. Ramone is a good student when he wants to be, but he'd rather be out on the football field with his friends and coaches. Jack loves history; he owns several historically accurate computer games and knows all of the big names from each period. Sarah is creative and outgoing—she's thinking about pursuing theatre after she graduates from high school.

But right now, they're all a little nervous; Mr. James is rumored to be tough; other students say that the work is hard, but that they learned a lot, whatever that means.

Mr. James gets to the room right as the bell rings. He sets his stuff down and says: "Hey there, everyone, welcome to American history. Our first unit is going to be on the Civil War."

"Great," Ramone thinks, "another unit about dead white guys. I hope homework from this class doesn't cut into practice."

"We're going to be using the content from that time period to develop our understanding of different perspectives on the same experience . . ."

Rachel thinks, "This doesn't sound like it's going to be on the AP test . . . is it too late to drop this class?"

". . . We'll be studying the Civil War and the different perspectives in an attempt to understand the human experience of 'conflict' and how the same event can be interpreted in many different ways. You'll be given 'characters,' who may or may not have actually existed, to role play."

Jack thinks, "What's the point? Facts are facts. I already know all about the Civil War."

". . . The final project will be a 15-minute video that you'll write and direct yourselves, about a situation in which your characters might have interacted."

"Yes," Sarah thinks, "I love improv. I'll just make it up as I go along."

"Your final product will be shown to the community. In the past, we've had parents, grandparents, administrators, and siblings attend—it's usually a pretty big group that comes out to see the pieces you'll be creating. Any questions? No? All right," Mr. James finishes, "Let's get to work."

Mr. James has been using Teaching Questions to teach this class for a couple of years, even though it means a lot of work and flexibility on his part. The Thinking Questions that Mr. James is going to ask in this unit will:

1. Ask students to synthesize what they think they already know along with new information that he will provide;
2. Allow the students to figure out an answer(s) for themselves (they will have to Re-view what they think they know and create a brand-new answer);
3. Allow for a spectrum of answers (Some answers will be "Righter" or "Wronger." Robust "thinking" will include qualifiers such as "if . . ." or "then . . . ");
4. Have multiple "right" answers, as long as the rationale makes sense. Much higher-order thinking is based upon life experiences—with different experiences come different answers (that may still be correct); and
5. Elicit answers that are content rich and concept focused—students will use content to answer questions rather than just naming content facts.

The answers to TQs are ultimately experience based; when students explain their reasoning, they will eventually reference some prior, personal experience.

Thinking questions matter because they empower the learner to use and access more and more information, to view their past experiences as both powerful and limiting, and to develop "habits of mind" which will increase the quality of their lives (both today and in the future).

When students think, they connect their classroom learning to their lives outside of school, they connect multiple facts into a larger concept, and they become comfortable considering long-term goals and ideas. Caring about teaching thinking shows that you care about your students as human beings.

Students are ready and waiting for someone to lead them with joy and enthusiasm toward a relevant end-in-mind. They hope that their teacher has: the knowledge of why it matters, the skills to show how it is done and the dispositions to choose to model complex personal thinking for them on a daily basis.

But teaching thinking is difficult, and because of its dynamic nature may be considered an "art," and an artist never ceases to refine their technique.

Facts are not knowledge—knowledge is the personal spin a person puts on how those facts are related and construct a specific concept. Similarly, you can't teach thinking out of a can. You can't look it up on your smartphone. You have to dance with the facts, paint with the students' prior experiences, sing with the students' assumptions (which could be wrong or very limited), and sculpt with how everything is informed by their belief systems.

Thinking is a creative endeavor, whether you're teaching it or learning it.

This first part is divided into four chapters, all focused on the students as they tackle the big-picture issues. Chapter 1 follows Rachel as she learns about Thinking Question dispositions (the habits of mind that thinkers tend to have). In chapter 2, Jack begins connecting knowledge to symbols in an attempt to model different types of thinking and puts a purpose to thinking in specific ways. In chapter 3, Sara learns TQ skills, such as the use of cue words in questions. Finally in chapter 4, Ramone struggles with the eternal question, "Why do I have to know this?"

1

RACHEL'S STORY
Questions of Dispositions

Rachel's Story: Rachel is a great student. She does her assignments well and turns them in on time. She understands how the system works and checks all of the boxes. She understands that some students aren't as smart as she is—that's OK. She never really minds compensating for a poor group member every now and again. It's not their fault. But she doesn't understand how a student can be "smart" and still get Bs and Cs. Why don't they just do the work?

Mr. James' class is beginning to give her real trouble. She is worried that she won't have all of the answers for the questions on the upcoming AP test. They seem to be moving soooooo slowly, and none of her answers seem to be "right" or "wrong." How is she supposed to know any of the answers? She goes in to talk to him about her frustrations.

Mr. James is grading their most recent research papers when Rachel walks in. She sits down and asks, "Mr. James, I feel like I'm not learning enough to pass the AP test. When are we going to start learning?"

Mr. James puts the papers down and sits back. Then he asks, "Rachel, you're a very good student, and I know this class is hard for you. So let me ask you a question: 'What is the point of a good education?'"

"What do you mean?"

"I mean, why do you come to school? What do you expect to get out of this?"

"I don't know. I want to get into a good college."

"And after that? A good job? And after that, what?"

"I don't really know."

One of the dilemmas in American education is that educators have no clear and agreed-upon purpose for what we are to accomplish. Everyone has their own ideas and therefore we lack a common focus as to our purpose. Is it to get students into a top college, as Rachel thinks, for better job prospects and more money? Is it to prepare students for the workforce (business would like this one!), to teach technical skills and vocabulary? These are both very marketable options, and could appeal to many students.

But does that apply to all students? What about the other students? The ones that aren't going to be going to Fortune 500 companies, who don't want to go to college? What about the stay-at-home parents, the self-starters, or the students that just don't know what they want yet? What's the point of an education for them? Shouldn't the goal of education be a little broader than preparing for a job and/or career?

In this book, the purpose of education is to "create self-actualized participants in a democratic society" (Kolis, 2011). Not only does the goal of self-actualization mean educating *everyone,* no matter where or who they are, but making this purpose clear and explicit would mean that our schools would help students develop lasting habits of mind and body rather than memorize trivia.

Much has been written on the topic of self-actualization, too much to do more than give a brief overview here. An education system focusing on helping students work toward self-actualization would allow students to:

1. Focus on continually "enhancing your quality of life"—a reflective and goal-focused habit.
2. Live with your passion in mind—makes hard work purposeful rather than drudgery.
3. Own your own learning—no excuses or blame.
4. Know your strengths and weaknesses—keep those strengths and work on those weaknesses.
5. Create and follow personal visions and goals—being purpose driven.
6. Transfer learning from one context to another—see the connections between the pieces.
7. Figure out stuff for yourself (options/choices), as rationally as possible, and
8. Contribute to others and society—the moral imperative of learning.

Fully self-actualized individuals would indeed behave with those ends in mind. The dilemma is if one teacher or one class could teach self-actualization, there would be little need for the 13 years of required education—even then, could we expect students to achieve this state at the age of 18? Of course not. Few people ever become self-actualized. You can't teach self-actualization: It's too big and too personal.

You can, however, interact with your students' Dispositions (actually, you begin to interact with their dispositions as soon as you sit in the same room with them). Dispositions are the lever by which a small amount of work can cause enormous changes.

Dispositions are the tendencies to think, believe and act in certain ways under certain circumstances (*Merriam-Webster*, 2002). They are the patterns of how someone chooses to think, the actions (or inactions) they take, and/or the extensions of what they most deeply believe.

There is a quote that describes dispositions perfectly: "You will always act in accordance with your deepest beliefs."

If you are unsure what your dispositions are, examine how you behave. Look to see where you spend your time, effort and resources (to meet your needs/be successful). That includes the things you say, the things you think but don't say, the things you buy, where you spend your time (at work and in play), and what skills you practice. Since everything you do is a choice (Glasser, 1998), your choices demonstrate to everyone what you truly care about—your tendency to act in certain ways under certain conditions.

Ultimately, your dispositions emerge from your deepest beliefs. Your dispositions are where the rubber meets the road; you can tell yourself whatever you want, but if you don't *act* in accordance with your beliefs, you don't really believe what you think you do. If you think and behave like a bad person, it doesn't matter what you believe about yourself: You are a bad person. You *always* act congruently with what you truly believe (even when you are unaware of those deep beliefs). And since learning is always a personal choice, the knowledge you have and the skills you chose to develop are extensions of those beliefs.

Mickey's Story: I love to bird hunt (or take a walk with my dog in some wild place with a gun. If I happen to shoot something, fine. If I don't, it's still fine). That means I have a hunting dog (and that means money). I have to create the time to go hunting (a time issue) and I had to learn about the birds in this area, places to actually hunt, seasons, bird habitat . . . I have had to prioritize my time, efforts and resources to do what I love. Those are all indicators of multiple beliefs: a conservationist viewpoint, a wellness belief and a belief that I can learn what I want to learn.

Focusing on teaching dispositions means to realize that individual learning is always a personal choice. The best any teacher can do is to provide experiences, thoughts and other perspectives in an environment where the learner is willing to consider learning (changing).

> Mr. James: "So, Rachel, what do you think your dispositions are? In what ways do you tend to act? What do you believe?"
>
> Rachel is quiet, thinking. Finally she says, "I think that, maybe, I think there's a right and a wrong answer to everything. I get frustrated when I don't have a clear answer."
>
> Mr. James: "That's a good place to begin—personal knowledge is important. With this class, I'm trying to teach you to learn on top of the knowledge. Is knowing the 'correct' answer learning? I mean, does memorizing the answers change how you think or behave?"

"Learning" (defined) is a change in thoughts, beliefs, or actions (*Merriam-Webster*, 2002). Without some sort of change, learning hasn't taken place. If students do not choose to use anything they have "learned" in the classroom in their lives outside the school setting, what have they spent all their time doing?

Consider this: If your students don't "tend to act" (have this particular disposition) like learners, what are the chances they'll make meaningful connections between their "real lives" and the classroom? If, however, you can present the right opportunities and experiences, a chance to be curious and try new things in a low-risk environment, you might be able to change "how they tend to act" in real life.

And being a learner is important. If someone "wants" to learn something, they are willing to give of their time, effort and resources to learn that thing—always. Interacting (successfully) with your students on the dispositions level allows you to help them make lasting changes in their lives.

So when we teach students "Thinking Questions," we are trying to help them change their dispositions (the way they tend to act). Just like in every discipline, there are specific dispositions that Thinking Questions tend to stress. Thinking Question dispositions include a willingness:

1. To Re-think what you know, believe and can do in the face of new experiences, facts or alternative beliefs;
2. To search for multiple right answers;
3. To seek out and use expert-level criteria when making important decisions;
4. To exhibit an action-orientation; and
5. To view other people's experiences as creative opportunities.

When teaching students to "think" explicitly, the idea is to help them replace their current thoughts, beliefs and actions with habits that are more nuanced, complex, sophisticated, robust, thoughtful, and holistic. Everyone is acting in ways they believe best meet their needs—even when life consequences show them otherwise. They need other thoughts, other ideas and other actions to change the outcomes—and they need help "learning" to make more effective decisions.

The point of "thinking" (aligned with purpose of education) is to "create self-actualized participants in a democratic society." Students are not our prisoners when it comes to learning—they, and only they, decide what they learn (change) based upon personal "thinking," and a focus on teaching dispositions allows for the greatest "learning."

Rachel: "OK . . . I guess. But what about the AP test?"

Mr. James: "I know you're stressed about the test, and I know that change isn't easy. It sounds like you feel like I'm teaching learning instead of teaching history—would that be accurate?"

Rachel: "Yeah, I mean the test isn't going to ask me the same things you're asking me. I just don't see how it could help."

Mr. James: "OK. Tell you what: give me a month to convince you that this is valuable, that you can 'learn' history and get all the information you need to pass the test. That in fact, the two things go hand in hand. Can you give me that? If at the end of the month you feel like you're not getting the information, I'll make you a personal study guide for every unit."

Rachel: "OK. I guess so."

Mr. James gets up and opens the door for Rachel. "Thanks for stopping by. Keep asking questions—it helps keep me honest."

Trusting someone to put you in situations where you can actually learn something important is tough; you're trusting another person with your successes and failures, your whole future self. Yes, focusing on dispositions is risky—but on the other hand, so is continued failure or continuing to do the same thing over and over again in a rapidly changing world. Focusing on teaching dispositions is the lever for helping people come to understand that they control their lives.

In chapter 2 we meet Jack, who is a self-proclaimed "expert" on the Civil War.

2

JACK'S STORY
Questions of Knowledge

While memorizing content is not the goal of Thinking Questions, content matters because thinking requires something to think about—and in most classrooms and learning opportunities that includes content. But if our education is going to act toward a purpose (the big picture/purpose being self-actualization, the small picture/goal being changing the way students tend to act in each discipline), we need to educate on three fronts, not just content (knowledge).

We need to teach Dispositions (we talked about that last chapter), Knowledge (this chapter), and Skills (next chapter), in discipline-specific ways. This chapter is about the Knowledge prong of our three-prong attack.

Jack's Story: Jack thinks of himself as a Civil War enthusiast. He knows the dates for all the important events and has a head for names. It's just one of the things that he's really good at. He also loves Civil War historical fiction, where fictional characters interact with real historical figures, and he loves picking out factual errors that other students make and adding obscure or little-known facts about the topics Mr. James is teaching about.

Sometimes just as Jack is about to offer more specific information, Mr. James will move on—even if the information is relevant (to Jack). Doesn't Mr. James want his students to know all this neat stuff? Rachel said that her meeting with Mr. James helped, so as Mr. James is locking his door before going home, Jack ambushes him.

Jack pounces: "Hey, Mr. James—can I ask a quick question about class?"

Mr. James looks at his watch, and says, "Sure, Jack, what's up?"

"It just seems like we skip over a bunch of stuff. I love the Civil War, and I know that we're not getting super in depth with everything—there's a bunch of stuff that you're not talking about that's really interesting; are we ever going to talk about all those things?"

Mr. James unlocks his door and turns on the lights, saying, "Good question. Come on in. Let's sit for a minute. The simple answer is, yes, we probably will. The more complex answer is that we have some other big concepts to talk about in combination with all those facts and stories. Now let me ask you a question: Is the information that we're talking about in class—just the information—different or better or worse than the information that you can get online?"

"I guess it's about the same."

"You're right, of course—but my job isn't just to communicate facts. My job is to teach you how to think—actually think—in a discipline-specific way, which is different than being a storyteller or a fact-checker. Do you see what I mean?"

Knowledge is important. Having the discipline-specific facts is what allows teachers to communicate content to their students, and what allows professionals to communicate with other professionals, and students to pass standardized tests. Consider "teacher-proof" courses, classes designed like a cookbook so every teacher achieves a standard result: students that "know" the specific facts. For many teachers, this is fine. It's easier to teach the content and only the content.

But facts only help people learn (change how they think, believe, or act) if those people know how to think.

Being a TQ teacher implies more than knowing facts related to your discipline; it means knowing how to convey those facts to others in ways that will enhance their lives. Science teachers must know science facts *as well as* know how to teach science so that the entire process improves student's lives. History teachers must be students of history *and* know how to teach history in ways that make history relevant. It's also why many colleges and universities don't require their faculty to have teaching degrees; by the time a student gets to college, the assumption/expectation is that students should have the thinking and learning thing down.

CHAPTER 2

"And that's why your lessons are so weird?"

Mr. James laughs. He walks to the whiteboard and starts drawing something. "Well, I'd probably put it a different way, but yes, that's why the lessons are so weird. Since I—as your teacher—can't make you learn anything you don't want to learn, I try to construct experiences wherein it will benefit you to think in certain ways." He steps away from the board. On it he's scribbled:

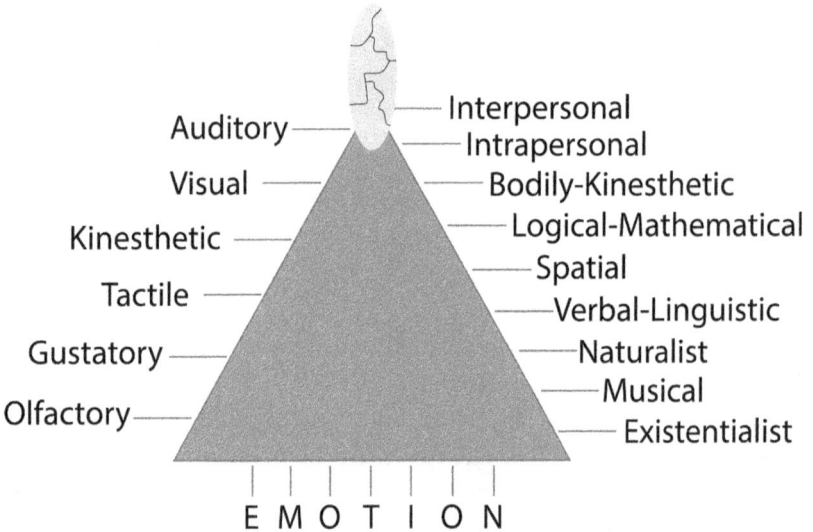

Auditory — Interpersonal
— Intrapersonal
Visual — Bodily-Kinesthetic
Kinesthetic — Logical-Mathematical
— Spatial
Tactile — Verbal-Linguistic
Gustatory — Naturalist
— Musical
Olfactory — Existentialist

E M O T I O N

"This is sort of how I think about it."

We are who we are, and we think how we think because of our experiences, nothing more. To understand and influence student thinking we have to provide our students with deliberate and powerful experiences. The model that Mr. James has drawn represents one "experience."

Throughout the course of the book we'll be explaining, picking apart, and adding to this model, starting with just one experience:

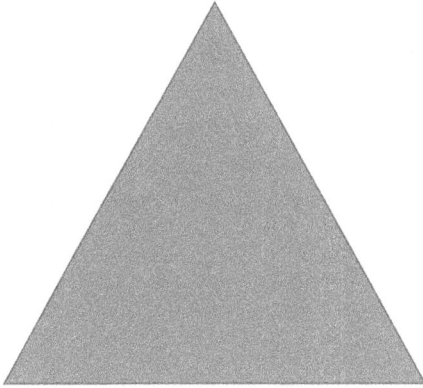

and going all the way to Action where students create their own understandings.

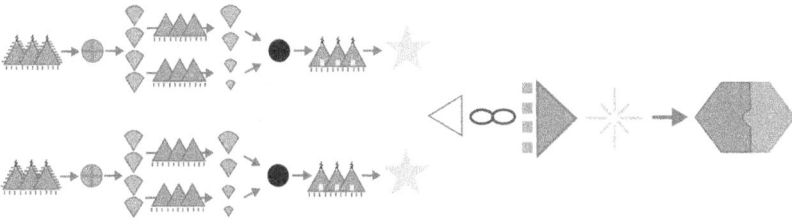

Mr. James asks, "So, Jack, what is the thing about the Civil War that really gets you excited?"

Jack replies, "Well, I really love the reenactments. My dad took me to one like a year ago and it was the best! We camped out, ate Civil War food, sang songs from the time period and then fought a mock battle. It was a fantastic weekend!"

Mr. James responds, "Nice. Reenactments are cool because you get to use all the information you've learned as well as give you a reason to learn more information."

Knowledge is useful (and worth remembering) when you put it to use. Measuring matters when you are building something, cooking something or making something to scale. Theory matters when you have to fix something on your own.

A good bike mechanic knows all the components of a bike. She knows how it all fits together and how each part works (by itself and with all the other parts). If you're constructing an experience for your students, shouldn't you know how the experience is constructed and what it will do?

Models allow us to "see" (visualize and "know") both the big picture and the pieces. Models provide a visual where there really isn't one and that visual allows us to "see the complexity" and then Intentionally and Explicitly plan for certain types of thinking to take place.

All models have a key weakness, namely, that they are models—they are *not* the real thing (they are representations). All models are too simplistic; they lack scale and depth and connections between the pieces. Letters, numbers, signs, shapes, and music notes are representations, not reality. The letters *d . . . o . . . g* are just that—three letters that we use to represent a living thing—a dog.

And what they represent is always personal. Your understanding and perspective of "dog" is different than mine. That means everyone has their own "working definition" for almost any concept (flavored by our personal experiences). So we say the same thing, and think we are in agreement when in reality we have totally different working definitions of the same concept.

While symbols are not the real thing, they do allow us a beginning point in understanding how complex a question is for our students (in terms of thinking, prior experiences and future thinking). They provide a beginning point for 1) thinking, 2) planning, and 3) assessments.

Diagrams (models) also show the big picture—and how the little pieces fit. They are the diagram in the "instructions" along with the step-by-step written words. The importance of diagrams is apparent for anyone who's purchased anything from Ikea (I'd have no stable furniture were it not for those drawings upon those flimsy pieces of paper).

An explicit symbol (picture) of what thinking entails also provides a strategy for dealing with and understanding "wrong" answers. It allows us to find out where the learner got lost (what they are really thinking) and how to help them Re-think what they know (everyone is responsible for their own understanding). Thinking "incorrectly" does in fact matter, either right now or at some point in the future.

Models help students visualize their own "thinking," and that helps them own their own learning. Thinking itself is developmental; we are all limited and blessed by our experiences, our genetic abilities and our developmental learning trajectory. Seeing thinking allows people to decide for themselves if there might be other, more productive ways of thinking.

One strength of a developmental outlook is that since we come back to the same big ideas over and over again, not everything has to be "perfect" at that time and place. We *grow* into our understandings.

Mickey's Story: When our oldest son was in first grade he had a wonderful teacher. During our first meeting with her she talked about how to be supportive when helping our son learn to write.

She used the word "temporary" (versus "inventive") spelling. She liked that term better because many adults were getting hung up on that "inventive" term—they did not want their child to "invent" spellings that were wrong.

"Temporary" also means developmentally appropriate. There is a time and place for certain kinds of tasks. And as they grow over time (developmentally) they would grow into correct spellings.

She was right on the mark and her students were not overwhelmed with developmentally inappropriate details!

The idea of coming back to the same idea over and over again (each time adding more complex and more specific information) is called scaffolding. Scaffolding works as a curriculum model because it removes some common assumptions when it comes to learning: 1) Not everything has to be totally right at every moment in time—it just has to be developmentally appropriate (for now); 2) not all information has to be taught all at once the big (important) ideas in every field crop up time after time; and 3) just because we love the details does not make them relevant to our students.

Thinking is complex business, but just saying something is complex is not very helpful (either you "get it" or you don't) and certainly not learningful. Thinking in certain ways is also a pattern and the more complex the thinking, the more it benefits everyone when the complexity is acknowledged and made explicit. Models (diagrams) are one "tool" that we can use to empower students to "think" for themselves.

In our next chapter we meet Sarah who knows how to play the schooling game, but doesn't take much seriously.

3

SARAH'S STORY
Questions of Skills

Sarah's Story: Sarah is a performer through and through. She is loud and funny, and loves being the center of attention. Both students and teachers like her, and she can often get by without giving her all because she's so quick witted and likable. She's an OK student and she's OK with it—she enjoys school because that's where all of her friends are. She is known to say things like, "Cs get degrees."

On this particular day, Sara and the rest of the class are working on the question, "What are some common characteristics between the way all wars begin?" (an analysis thinking question). Mr. James is taking down their suggestions on the board. Ramone has just come up with "economic pressure," when Sarah raises her hand and calls out:

"MR. JAMES, I'M SO BORED. WE ALREADY KNOW ALL OF THIS."

The class laughs, and Mr. James laughs and says, "I get the feeling you're trying to tell me something. You guys feel like you know the content pretty well?" The class mumbles an affirmative except for a "YES!" from Sarah. "OK, Sarah, now you've done it. You've drawn my ire. Question time. You know the material; that's great. Sarah, what are the things you have to know when you're about to go into a performance?

"You have to know your lines and your blocking,"

"OK, great, and what do you have to be able to DO? As in, what skills make it possible to perform your lines and blocking?"

"You mean, like projecting and being able to speak clearly?"

"Right. That's what we're working on right now: You guys have the content down—your lines are memorized, and you've written down your blocking. Now we're working on our skills. Except instead of theatre, we're talking about thinking. And how do you sharpen your skills? Ramone, what do you think? How do you sharpen your skills?"

Ramone is a little startled to be dragged into the discussion. "I don't know."

Mr. James: "Oh, you don't, do you? Where do you go after school every day?"

Ramone: "Uh, practice." He gets it. "Oh."

Mr. James: "And why do you practice so much?"

Ramone is smiling now. "You practice so you don't have to think about doing whatever you're practicing. Coach says that you don't even start to really enjoy playing the game until you stop having to think about your body doing its job."

"That's what I think too," says Mr. James.

A professional in any discipline has skills, which are defined by *Merriam-Webster* (2002) as "the ability to use one's knowledge effectively and readily in execution or performance." Skills are the enactment of knowledge (if the knowledge is explicit). This blending of knowledge and skill is the difference between a worker, a craftsman and an artist—in any field.

Skills don't arise spontaneously out of knowledge. Rather, they are the result of practice, repetition, and trial and error. You don't become an artist without laborious development of sculpting technique, and you don't become a thinker without practice and repetition.

Thinking Questions (TQs) ask the learner to think in specific ways for a particular purpose (a specific end-in-mind). These thinking skills, just like the tools of any trade, have names, are specific, and are most effective when they're used in the correct circumstances.

Each Thinking Question requires the use of a specific cue word for the task at hand and each TQ is based upon prior TQs as well as the foundation for those yet to come (a systems point of view). We'll go over the specific skills in the upcoming chapters.

Answering TQs requires a specific set of skills, but so does constructing and *asking* them. Students won't use thinking skills at all, let alone the correct ones, if the teacher doesn't know how to elicit them.

All Thinking Questions share specific characteristics (the skills of the TQs):

1. They are all open-ended questions. That means there are multiple correct responses (some of course more correct than others).
2. They each use a "cue word" which specifies the type of thinking that is being required. Change the cue word and you change the TQ! (There is a big difference between "list the pieces" and "rank the pieces.")
3. Student answers provide the "data" to know if you can move on or need to Re-visit prior thinking.

Learning the skills of asking TQs allows the teacher to create Thinking Questions Intentionally and Explicitly to meet a learning goal (remember the definition of learning—a change in thought, beliefs or action). The right TQs in the right sequence helps everyone in the class become more explicit about their thinking and even allows for students to help each other—when help is needed.

Asking TQs requires a degree of intentionality and explicitness that must be practiced and is not usually seen in most classrooms. If we teach (and students learn) the knowledge, skills and dispositions of the TQs, they will be prepared for the "How's" and "What's" of life. Thinking is not random, not happenstance, and not serendipity, which means it can be practiced and improved.

One powerful end-in-mind for great teachers, parents, coaches and mentors is to empower others in such a way as to make themselves dispensable! The point of *Thinking Diagrams* is to empower our learners to meet their own needs (in a rapidly changing world). That requires skills (rather than hope)!

Teaching (and learning) is a lifelong process. Not everything has to be taught all at once. What matters is to teach skills and knowledge and the dispositions—in age (and experience) appropriate ways.

Skills are specific; it's clear when someone does it well, and you see the change in behavior right now. That also makes them easy to assess. Complexity lies in that skills lead somewhere—they are not that important all unto themselves. Skills are important because when a bunch of small skills are combined, they allow you to DO something interesting and complex.

Finally, in the next chapter we meet Ramone, who asks the most challenging teacher question of all: "Why do I have to know this stuff?"

4

RAMONE'S STORY
Questions of Relevance

Ramone's Story: Ramone plays football. He's really good, and gets most of what he needs from the team. His coaches are his mentors and role models; most of his friends are on the team and they talk about football all the time. The team encourages him to keep his grades up (otherwise he can't play) and if he does well enough in the next two seasons he might even get some money to go to college. He mostly tries to do his school work and keep his head down. He grew up next door to Sarah, one of the few friends he has outside of football.

Mr. James finishes talking about skills and looks around. Ramone is doodling. Mr. James notices. "Ramone," he says, "you don't look convinced."

"Uh, well, no, I mean that sounds great," he says. "I just don't know when I'm going to use any of this, you know?"

"What do you mean, Ramone?"

"Well, I mean, I get like practicing skills in football; you practice to get better so you can win. I'm not going to be a historian and I don't even really like history, so I don't really know why I have to know this."

"Ahh," says Mr. James, "now that is an excellent question." His eyes light up as he begins to speak.

Learning (the deep and powerful kind) involves: Dispositions (the ways students tend to act), Knowledge (the content) and the Skills (how to use knowledge). That's a good start but an important piece is still missing: What is in it for our students to learn (change)? What makes our topic relevant?

Relevance is the cornerstone of motivation. When things are relevant (to me) it means I will give of my time, my effort and my resources to do those things that I believe best meet my needs.

Relevance is always personal—like knowledge and learning. My reason to learn something is going to be different than yours. What Ramone is struggling with is a relevance issue—the big teaching and learning question: "*Why do I have to know this?*"

So, what matters to our students? Does the paper you just assigned matter? To whom? Why should it? If the only reason your students consider an assignment important is to avoid punishment, that's a problem. We frequently assign things that are important (only) to us and then wonder why students do not find them relevant (important enough to actually do).

Teachers are highly educated. We work in a field where most teachers believe that more education will increase students' quality of life (hopefully). What we do not know is what the future will hold for our students—what jobs will be available, how long those jobs and careers will be viable, and what society will actually value.

Those uncertainties mean we "predict" that what we teach today will in fact matter (be relevant) in the future. When students "trust" the teacher, that means they also trust the teacher's predictions about what will make them better (a big responsibility).

Students are living in a world where everything competes for their time—sports, friends, activities, social media, family. Teachers (and school assignments) are in competition with everything else students find interesting (and worth their time, effort and resources). In order for tasks to be considered "relevant" by our students they must be both of the following:

1. Real (falls within their timeframe of caring).
For many of our students the here and now is the "future." They might be willing to change a behavior for something going on this weekend (maybe) but things like "when you go to college," "get a job," and "get married," are too far in the future to impact their behavior today for the majority of our students.

2. True (has a high probability of actually taking place in the future) (Kolis, 2011).

When an experience is both Real and True, it is more likely that students will be motivated to learn (change). But change (learning) is hard. We do what we do because we think it works for us. Our thoughts and/or actions have become habits, and learning means to replace one pattern of thought and/or behavior with another—and that takes time, effort and resources to accomplish.

Since learning can be challenging, support helps (emotionally, intellectually, physically, socially and morally). The key learning idea is to provide the right kind of support at the right time. That means support that is: 1) not too much or too little, 2) not too soon or too late, and 3) not too easy or too hard. Support does not mean to do the task for them, give them the answer or remove the obstacles.

Support means to give them "just enough" help so they may continue their own learning journey. Trusting them enough to let them struggle through the challenging times shows them that you believe in them. It gives them the power to persevere. It also helps prepare them to be independent (later hopefully interdependent) human beings.

Relevance is all about "why" answers. Things that are seen as relevant allow people to commit themselves to the learning journey. If it matters to the individual, spending time, effort and resources becomes the means to the end, rather than an assignment to be completed.

"Why" answers are also the basis for the "How" and "What" answers (the detail answers). "Why" answers make "purpose" explicit—and that matters because creating the habits of mind with an explicit purpose allows each individual to create their own personal visions and goals.

Note: We have been talking a lot about "end-in-mind" thinking. To clarify, this is not about "What do you want to be when you grow up?" rather "What kind of person do you wish to become?" It is the difference between "I want to be a CEO when I grow up" versus "I want to be a kind, caring, loving, responsible, trustworthy, independent (interdependent later), and respectful human being."

The key to making learning relevant is to provide opportunities to learn developmentally appropriate stuff that will cumulatively add up to the desired end-in-mind.

Mickey's Story: My wife and I wanted our sons to grow up to be independent and proactive. That meant we had to allow them opportunities to grow into those characteristics.

When one of our sons was in second grade he got into trouble on the playground at school. His punishment was no more recess for the rest of the week. It was an appropriate punishment, but it really bothered him because he said he did not actually do the naughty behavior (and he loved recess).

So we told him the correct procedure (call the principal and make an appointment) to discuss the situation. We never thought he actually would—but he did in fact call and make that appointment. I went with him for support, but told him I wouldn't speak because it was his deal.

So we went and the principal was very kind. He asked what happened, how his friends would feel if he was not punished and what he might do differently the next time he was in that position. Our son addressed those issues and at the end a new solution was generated.

Recess and "fairness" were "relevant" to that son. He was willing to do the tasks required to address that need by himself with appropriate support. We did not "fix it" for him; we provided support that we hoped was developmentally appropriate.

And that is the challenge for finding "relevance" for all our students. What is relevant to one may not be relevant to all. Working with students as individuals helps us make learning *more* relevant (if not totally) at that time and place.

Making learning both real and true helps. To make TQs relevant to our students, we must *sell* (be passionately committed to) the following ideas:

1. The Explicit and Intentional use of Thinking Questions increases the chance (probability) of making a "good" decision (a good decision sounds like "I made the best decision I could at that time in that place knowing what I knew").

Helping our students create a powerful Habit of Mind (using TQs) will allow them to be "successful" in a rapidly changing world. Thinking—not a list of memorized facts—will be the coin of future success (personally as well as professionally).

In reality they already "think for themselves"; we just do not know what that thinking looks like or where it may be flawed. Since we do not teach "thinking" explicitly we also cannot be good teachers and coaches in that endeavor. We recognize it when we see it (they are a good "thinker") but we don't teach it intentionally.

2. Foster a "take them from where they are and move them along the learning continuum" perspective. We need to teach them where they are right now (meet their needs today, this minute) rather than prepare them for college, marriage, or the workforce (if we teach them in ways that meet their needs right now, they will be prepared for the future).

We live longer and longer and yet push our kids to graduate earlier and earlier. Life is not a race. Being potty trained first, graduating from high school early, skipping grades—these do not guarantee life success. Those are "parent competitions" with little regard for setting students up for life success, life lived toward a purpose and the development of strong relationships with others and the world.

One beauty of a developmental perspective is that "learning activities" are always perfect (either they are doing it totally correct, or I now know what we need to learn next). In life outside of school most learning is in fact developmental—we rarely expect perfection. We expect to work toward perfection, always learning, always growing in our knowledge, our skills or our dispositions.

3. Our goal is to make ourselves dispensable. In terms of power that means we must keep what we must, share what we can and give what we dare. In life, we are not there when our students (or children) make their most important life decisions (sex, drinking, drugs, etc.), so we have to let them make their own decisions in developmentally appropriate situations (that means the consequences are age appropriate). Saving kids from consequences removes powerful learning opportunities.

In the "old days" kids played a lot of "sandlot" games. They actually played games without adults being present! They picked their own teams, adjusted the fields and made their own calls. There were arguments but kids also then learned how to resolve them by themselves (or take the ball and go home).

Play is learning, and adults need to let go and let the kids learn things for themselves—not like the old days but better than the old days. Learning is a risky business, which is what makes it powerful and meaningful. "Nothing ventured, nothing gained." You *accomplished something* when the end was in doubt.

4. Learning is a lifelong endeavor (learning defined as a "change in thoughts, beliefs or actions"). That means in the classroom the teacher needs to be the very best learner!

Learning includes knowledge, skills and dispositions. Learning is an adaptability as well as a moving-forward mind-set. Current thoughts, beliefs and actions act as placeholders for future thoughts, beliefs and actions.

Learning matters in all parts of our lives (jobs, relationships, roles, etc.). People continue to change based upon their development and experiences. The best learners put themselves into places where they can learn the most.

Mr. James is starting to wind down: "Does that make sense, everyone? I'm not trying to make you memorize a bunch of random facts, and I'm not trying to tell you what to think about them. What I am trying to do is get you to use, label, and sharpen the thinking skills you use every day. Just—in here—we're taking those skills and asking questions about history."

Sarah, Jack, Ramone, and Rachel are all nodding. Mr James: "Awesome. I know this is new for you guys. I tell you what. We have lots of stuff to do today already, but on Monday, how about I talk a little bit about how I plan things—show you the method to the madness. Does that sound OK? Great. Let's move on."

II

WHERE THINKING QUESTIONS BEGIN

Experience(s)

Sarah, Ramone, Jack, and Rachel are sitting at a table in class wait-ing for Mr. James. It's Monday, but doesn't feel like it—Mr. James has promised to do some explaining about how he teaches, and they're excited to shoot him down if they can.

He comes in right as the bell rings, throws his bag on his desk, and says: "I spent the whole weekend trying to come up with a good way to do this little session, and I think I'm going to start with a question: What makes you the way that you are?"

Sarah says, "Genetics."

Jack adds, "How you're raised. Nurture, I guess."

Rachel: "Your thoughts are you."

Ramone thinks a minute: "Your experiences."

Mr. James: "All of those are correct, but we're going to start with Ramone's answer. Your experiences."

According to *Merriam-Webster* (2002) "experience" is defined as the "practical contact with and observation of facts or events," which is a decent place to start talking about Thinking Questions (TQs).

Students enter our classrooms with a lifetime of prior experiences. What they have come to understand about the world through those experiences may be correct, inaccurate or totally wrong. It doesn't matter: Those experiences have shaped their thoughts, beliefs and actions (there is no reality, only perception). They *are* their experiences.

Constructing powerful learning experiences means putting students in "practical contact with and observation of facts and events" in ways that will allow them the opportunity to change how they behave, think or act in the face of those new experiences.

Great. Educators already do that, right? Movies, memorization, group projects, and jeopardy review are all experiences, right? Sure they are. But are they powerful enough to help students Re-think, Re-view, and Re-conceptualize what they think they already know? Most of the time they aren't; they tend to fade into the background.

We cannot provide *more* experiences than what they have already had to our students (they have a lifetime of those, and we get maybe five hours a week), so we have to make sure the experiences we can construct for them are powerful (more memorable, more learningful, of higher quality, more complex) in terms of thinking.

So what makes one experience more powerful (more memorable, more learningful, of higher quality, more complex) than another one?

Mr. James nods at each one. "Yeah, yeah, all of those are correct of course. Each of those things is a part of who you are. Let me change the question a little bit: What can make you change your mind about something? What can change the way you think about something?"

There's a pause.

"OK, here's an example: You've always liked dogs. You didn't grow up with cats; you grew up with dogs. What might convince you that cats are equally good pets? Could anything convince you?"

Rachel says, "I grew up with cats. I didn't like dogs until my neighbor got a German shepherd puppy—they named her Ali—she was the cutest little thing."

"Right," says Mr. James. "Would you have believed someone who told you that you'd like dogs just as much as you like cats?"

"I guess not."

Teacher-created experiences must also include very specific questions that push students outside their comfort zones (how they normally think and view reality) in an environment that supports risk taking (in terms of learning). We call these deep and powerful questions Thinking Questions.

Thinking Questions must push students to access more information than they usually would (we see what we want to see and hear what we want to hear). Thinking Questions are based on real-life, hands-on experiences *and* what you think you already know (read the story *Fish Is Fish* by Leo Lionni). Consider driving to work versus riding to work. Same event, different perceptions. That difference gives us the space to notice things we've never noticed before, reflect, and change our perspectives.

Mr. James draws something on the board.

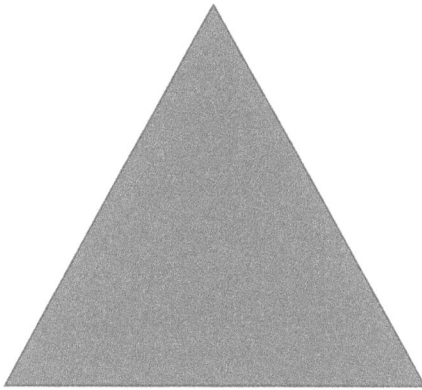

"I submit that your experiences are the foundation of what you know, believe and can do. I think that your genetics and experiences shape nearly everything about you, that you don't think or do anything that is unsupported by your experiences. Something as simple as whether you like dogs or cats is due ONLY to your genetics and your experiences with dogs and cats."

He turns to face the room. "Which means, if I'm going to teach— if I'm going to try to change the way you think, act, and believe—I need to provide more and/or more powerful experiences, because you won't believe me if I just tell you anything."

This next section introduces Thinking Questions, each with its own diagram which represents how an individual has to think to answer the question as well as cue words for each TQ. All Thinking Questions are: 1) open ended (have many correct responses), and 2) have a specific cue word that asks students to think in specific ways.

Chapter 5 addresses the use of Senses to broaden the amount of information the learner takes in and chapter 6 addresses the ways we process and connect those experiences with our prior experiences. Chapter 7 focuses on how our Mental Models and Emotion impact our experiences and chapter 8 shows how it all works together to develop our conceptual understandings. Finally chapter 9 addresses how the "art" of teaching thinking requires a "messy world" perspective.

Mr. James begins: "So what does an experience look like?"

5

SENSES

Mr. James begins, "The way I think about it, a single experience, like petting a dog or eating a cookie, looks like this." He points to the figure on the board:

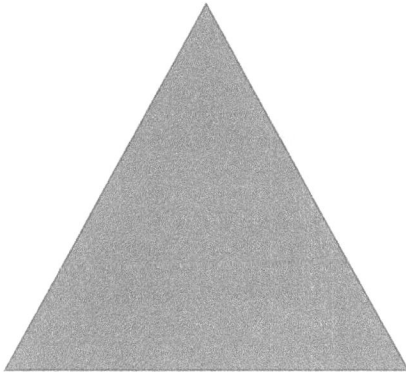

"But what is an experience? What components make up an experience?"

Rachel and Ramone say together: "Touch."

Sarah says, "What you see."

"Yes, that's right, and a great place to start—your senses."

Experiences start with our senses (at least for our public school–aged students). Our bodies have a natural three-dimensional inclination—we just like having 3-D experiences. Watch a child "play" and you'll observe them using almost all of their senses. The term *3-D* means that an object has weight, heft, texture, smell, taste, sound, color, and shape, and moves in certain ways. These types of 3-D experiences are called "concrete" experiences and in terms of learning are the strongest and most personal.

Sense Thinking Questions are the most basic level of Thinking Question and the first set of vocabulary of our model. Our senses are the most basic "portal" we have for receiving information, and asking Sense TQs can help students form intentional concrete experiences—the difference between looking at a picture of a "dog," and going to a dog park to touch, observe, and smell (maybe not taste) "dog" (the dog park being a concrete experience).

Developmentally, we later learn to think abstractly, but until we do (sometime in our early 20s), concrete experiences make up a tremendous amount of what we "know" about the world. This sense information is the basis for all of our thinking. We know best what we've experienced for ourselves.

Which is why we have to have the vocabulary to construct those concrete, 3-D experiences; we have to let students "play" before we start to teach. And to get our money's worth (in terms of creating the most powerful learning from those concrete experiences), the more of the following senses we ask them to notice the better.

Mr. James begins adding to the experience triangle until it becomes

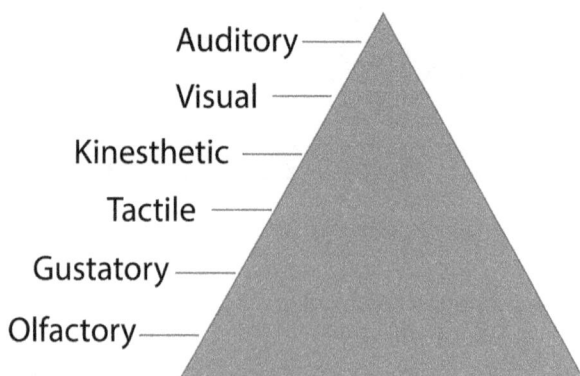

Auditory
Visual
Kinesthetic
Tactile
Gustatory
Olfactory

Diagram Explanation: One triangle represents one experience with something. The "sticks" on the left side represent our senses—the ways we get information into our beings. Every individual uses some senses more than others (more is better in terms of information).

1. Visual (sense of sight)—our sense of sight inputs data into our brains by translating light into images and colors. This includes color, lightness, darkness, form, depth, shape, and focus.

Thinking Question Visual Cue Words:

See	Look like	Shape
Styles	Colors	Size
Patterns of light/dark		Proportions

Note: Each list of Cue Words is not exhaustive! The more you work with these lists the more cue words you might use.

2. Auditory (sense of sound)—our sense of sound inputs data into our brains by translating perceived sound waves as electrical impulses. This includes pitch, rhythm, timbre, and volume.

Thinking Question Auditory Cue Words:

Sounds	Hear	Loud
Pitch	Frequency	Rhythm

3. Kinesthetic (sense of movement)—our sense of movement puts information into our brains such as pressure, balance, and movements. Kinesthetic here has a large muscle-orientation. This includes walking, running, acting, jumping, and role playing.

Thinking Questions Kinesthetic Cue Words:

Jump	Bounce	Fly
Sink	Roll	Chop
Dash	Dance	Gallop
Leap	Kick	Mime

4. Tactile (sense of touch)—our sense of touch puts information into our brains such as pressure, heat, cold, pain, soft, hard, rough, and smooth. Touching objects is fundamental to learning, especially early on (thus the intrigue of children's museums).

Thinking Question Tactile Cue Words:

Feels like	Texture	Rough
Smooth	Heavy	Light
Cold	Hot	Twist

5. Olfactory (sense of smell)—our sense of smell reaches directly into our emotions and memory (think of dirt or perfume). Frequently when we describe smells we say, "This reminds me of (my grandmother's house, a trip, a boy/girlfriend/partner)."
Thinking Question Olfactory Cue Words:

Smells like	Fragrant	Sweet
Stink	Foul	Detect
Whiff	Inhale	Sniff

6. Gustatory (sense of taste)—our sense of taste inputs data into our brains by translating taste into sweet, salty, bitter and sour (closely related to smell). Very frequently we compare tastes (tastes like chicken) which are culturally biased, because we have not developed a large vocabulary for describing tastes generally.

Individual fields where taste is important have more specific terms like *malty, hoppy, bitter, sweet, earthy, tinny.*
Thinking Question Gustatory Cue Words:

Tastes like	Flavors	Spicy
Sweet	Salty	Sour
Bitter	Savory	

Note: For Sense Thinking Questions the key is to have students *describe what they observe* (not the conclusions they draw from what they see). For example if you give them a pencil and ask them to make observations about what they see, they will frequently say "pencil" rather than make observations such as "it is five inches long, it is yellow, and it has five sides."

Sometimes when asking students to make observations, using more open-ended Cue Words suffices. These allow students to access any Sense, which may be problematic and yet gives them choice.

Thinking Question Generalized Cue Words:

Observe   Notice
Detect   Describe

We frequently do not have good language to describe our experiences (taste and smell are notoriously difficult). It appears so basic that we jump right to Conclusions rather than the Observations (think Sherlock Holmes). Jumping to conclusions is natural—knowing a pencil is a pencil is not wrong, just not the point of the exercise. The key for making Observations is to learn to notice the unnoticed.

What we (each of us as individuals) observe is the foundation of how we think and what we know. Our life experiences lay the foundation for our thoughts, our beliefs and our actions. We want our students to develop the language and thinking skills to describe simple and familiar objects so that we can apply the same principles to more complex objects and situations which they might not already "know."

As we get older we also have a tendency to notice what we want to notice and ignore other observations. Observations matter because they determine the quality of our experiences and how much information we will be able to recall in the future. The key aspect for teaching students how to make observations is to help them learn to use more of their senses on a regular basis. Information matters when it comes to thinking.

Classroom Examples:

1. Describe a strawberry using as many senses as possible.
2. What do you notice about the uniform of a Civil War soldier?
3. What did you observe about the people at the awards ceremony?
4. What did you see when you looked at the "couple" at the mall?
5. Describe what a well-constructed mask feels like.

Jack raises his hand and says, "I guess I see what you are saying; there's a difference between reading a Civil War story and eating

Civil War–era food at a reenactment. I get that. But I already know that. That's not a sense; that's something else."

Mr. James says, "You're absolutely right. Your senses are how you take in new information. Processing something you already know—or think you know—is something else."

6

PROCESSING

Mr. James continues: "While our senses are the most basic way we form experiences, they aren't the only way. I'm going to add a little something to our diagram here."

He adds to the diagram:

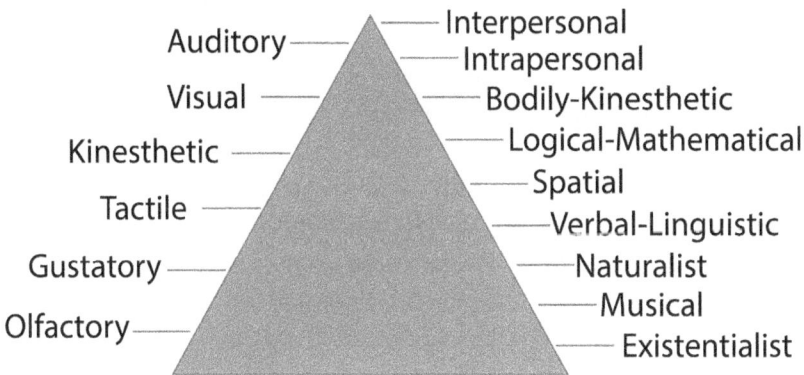

Diagram Explanation: The triangle represents one experience. It includes our senses (the left side) and now also how we process that information. When we process information we think about it in certain ways (the sticks on the right side) and connect the new experience to prior experiences.

Mr. James tells the following story: "My wife is a professional musician, which means we go to many performances. When we leave and talk about the performance, sometime it's like we were at different events; even though we were there together watching and listening to the same performance, we understand it in very different ways.

"Experiences are not just the information that gets into our brains from our senses. My wife and I processed the concert in different ways; we each used our unique set of Intelligences to process the experience."

Processing our observations means how we "think about" the information we took in (connections, relationships). We personalize the data we noticed (our senses) and since each person is an individual, we each emphasize some areas more than others. Processing observations includes the relationships we create with and between experiences and also how we connect those new experiences to our prior experiences.

While we are genetically predisposed to process information in specific ways, we each have all of the intelligences, albeit with varying strengths and weaknesses. The more ways of processing information we access, the more robust the experience, and the easier the experience is to recall and the greater the quantity of information we can access later.

So on the left we have our senses—the portals through which we receive information. On the right side we have the Multiple Intelligences (MI) (Gardner, 1983; Armstrong, 1993) by which we tend to process that information. One is not necessarily subordinate to the other—without senses we have no information, and without our Multiple Intelligences (processes), we have no way to relate the information to other information or prior experiences.

Processing Questions allow us to validate and access students' prior experiences, and to use each new experience as a foundation to reflect on other experiences, both new and old (How does this connect to what you've already experienced? What similar experiences have you had like this?).

Processing in groups is one powerful reason why working with others can be so helpful: Everyone adds their own specific way of processing to the experience. You processed the experience in your way, and so did I. Together we now each have access to more information than we would by ourselves. The "sticks" on the right side of the diagram also provide students with a vocabulary with which to share their perspective with others.

1. Interpersonal—this intelligence focuses on how we relate to others, your sensitivity to the moods, feelings, temperaments and motivations of others, and your willingness to cooperate to work as a group of individuals. Interpersonal intelligence goes beyond noticing those things about others to "being swayed" by them when making decisions.
Thinking Question Interpersonal Cue Words:

Others think   Others perceive
Others' experiences, feelings, and/or perspectives

2. Intrapersonal—this intelligence stresses knowledge of self, the willingness and frequency of introspection, and the ability to self-reflect without those "rose-colored glasses." Intrapersonal intelligence includes knowledge about one's personal strengths and weaknesses, uniqueness, and the ability to predict one's own reactions and thoughts.
Thinking Question Intrapersonal Cue Words:

How do you think about this?   How might this affect you?
How does this make you feel?   What are your strengths and weaknesses?
What is your perspective?   What does this mean to you?

3. Bodily-Kinesthetic—this intelligence includes the idea of being movement and touch driven. It includes the capacity to handle objects skillfully (making things), as well as dancing, acting, and sports. People who are Bodily-Kinesthetic intelligent communicate experiences and thoughts through movement, or creating objects which are meant to be felt.
Thinking Question Bodily-Kinesthetic Cue Words:

How would you express this with movements?   Feels like
How does this feel (tactilely)?
What movements do you associate with this experience?

4. Logical-Mathematical—this intelligence includes a focus on relationships (between items, not necessarily between people). These relationships include ideas of logic, abstractions, reasoning, numbers, critical thinking, cause and effect, correlation, sequence, and predictions.

Thinking Question Logical-Mathematical Cue Words:

If . . . , then . . .	Relationship	Sequence
Proportion (always, sometimes, never)	Uses	
Pattern		

5. Spatial—this intelligence stresses the ability to create two- and three-dimensional representations. It focuses on the ability to visualize with the mind's eye, see things from a different perspective (top, bottom, side, above . . .), and the ability to communicate experiences and thoughts through those 2- and/or 3-D representations.

Thinking Question Spatial Cue Words:

Made of	Represent	Shapes
Design features	Perspective	Rotate

6. Verbal-Linguistic—this intelligence focuses on words and languages, reading, writing, telling stories, vocabulary, definitions, and poetry. The key is to communicate experiences/thoughts through words.

Thinking Question Verbal-Linguistic Cue Words:

Story	Words	Sentence
Definition	Poem	Define

7. Naturalist—this intelligence sees everything connected in a world-system. Included ideas are classification, categories, niches, relationships, and structure and function.

Thinking Question Naturalist Cue Words:

Like (similar)	Niche	Group
Relationships	Web	Connections

8. Musical—this intelligence involves sounds, rhythms, tones, pitch, and how you hear things. People strong in this intelligence communicate their experiences and/or thoughts through sounds (not words).

Thinking Question Musical Cue Words:

Sounds like	Rhythm	Melody
Beat	Timbre	Pitch

9. Existentialist—this intelligence focuses on deep meanings (of life, tragedies, etc.), philosophy, and spirituality. The focus here in on the biggest picture possible (not all the small details), how everything works together toward some sort of end-in-mind.

Thinking Question Existential Cue Words:

Why	Meaning	How do the pieces work together

Each individual has their own MI strengths and weaknesses. We *prefer* some ways of processing our experiences more than others. Asking students to explicitly notice characteristics for each experience allows them to reinforce those preferred ways of thinks AND develop their areas of weakness.

Processing includes: your prior experiences (what you already think you know) and the lens you use to view new experiences. Sharing "processing" information allows everyone to increase the information about that experience. Since everyone is experiencing the same thing, sharing different perspectives enriches the experience for everyone. The experience would then include your own relationships and connections as well as those of others who process information differently, resulting in a win-win learning episode.

Classroom Examples:

1. What rhythms do you notice when you hear these sounds?
2. How does the structure of a strawberry fill a niche?
3. What stories do you have that connect to this experience?
4. What pattern might there be when you drop this ball?
5. When you saw our classmate get that big award, what thoughts went through your mind?

Mr. James looks at his watch: "Whoa, we've spent way too much time on this today. We'll pick the conversation up again tomorrow. For now—back the the Civil War. Ramone, can you tell us where we left off?"

MENTAL MODELS
AND THE POWER
OF EMOTION

Tuesday. Mr. James is about to start the lesson. He begins, "We spent a lot of time talking about the diagram yesterday. The more I think about it, the more I think it might be useful for you all if we can keep it visible. So let's keep this diagram around. We'll just move it over here. . ."

He erases the big diagram, which had been left on the board from Monday, and draws a smaller version in the corner of the board.

"Who can remind me what makes up an experience?"

Ramone: "Senses, and different ways of processing."

"That's great, Ramone. We're calling those different ways of processing Multiple Intelligences, or MIs. Today, we're going to add something else."

Mr. James adds a small lens at the top of the existing diagram, turning it into

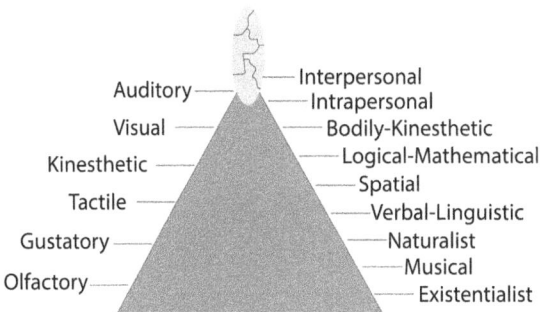

Auditory — Interpersonal
— Intrapersonal
Visual — Bodily-Kinesthetic
Kinesthetic — Logical-Mathematical
— Spatial
Tactile — Verbal-Linguistic
Gustatory — Naturalist
— Musical
Olfactory — Existentialist

"And one other thing here at the bottom."
Adding one other thing, it becomes:

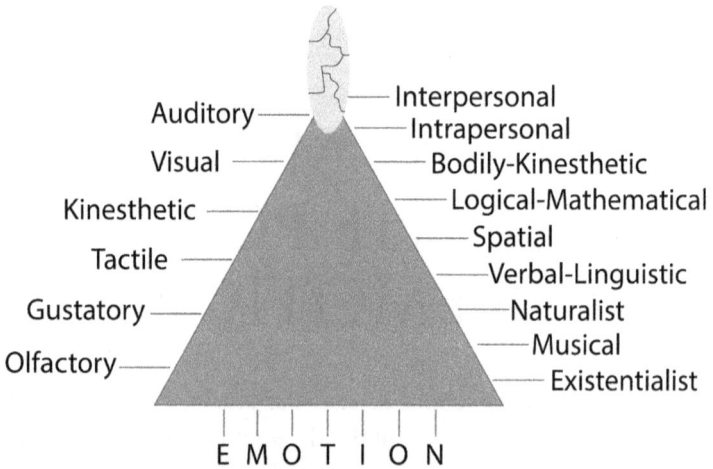

"That little lens at the top represents your paradigm, or mental model. That's the lens through which you see the world, which is at the top of the diagram there because both what you process and what you sense inform and are viewed only through your lens of life.

"Below that, at the base, that represents your emotions. Every experience you have is colored heavily by your emotions. Both of which lead us perfectly into our activity for the day."

Mr. James asks his students to imagine they are in Rowlett's Station, Kentucky, for a small skirmish between the North and the South. He randomly hands out short biographies of people who were at the event when it took place. Whites, blacks, preachers, businessmen, farmers, Union supporters and Confederate support-ers. . . . He shows them an eight-minute reenactment video and asks them to talk about what they think their experience would have been like.

Each individual is genetically predisposed to use specific senses and multiple intelligences more or less frequently than others. The reality is that how we view any experience is even more complex than just those variables. We also bring our own personal Mental Models (Senge, 1990) or Paradigms (Kuhn, 1970) to those experiences.

Because each human is such an individual and perceives reality in their own way, you could say that there is no reality, only perception. We perceive each experience not from an objective point of view; rather we view each experience through our lens of life.

Our lenses (mental models or paradigms) are created from:

1. Our context—how we grew up, what we saw modeled for us, life experiences such as travel, resources, books, culture, time, place, resources, and relationships all contribute to the lenses we create.
2. Who we are genetically (as we get old enough to form our own lenses), and
3. The interactions between the two.

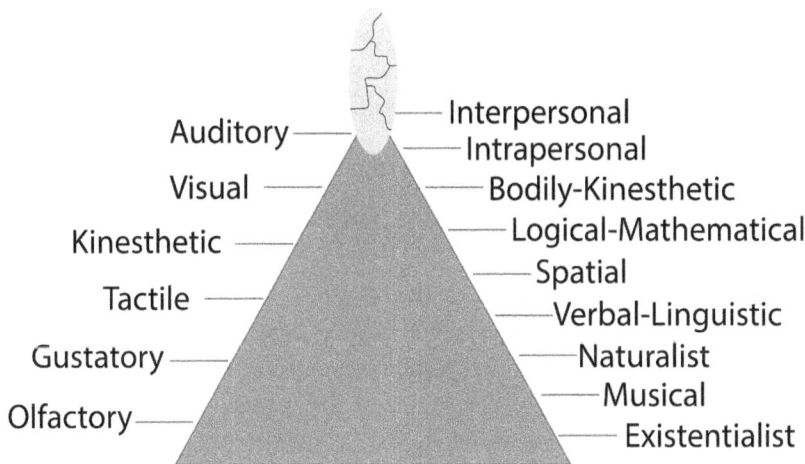

Diagram Explanation: For each experience we use our senses (sticks on the left), and process that information in our own specific ways (sticks on the right). Every experience is also personalized by the lens of life (lens on the top) which an individual chooses (sometimes) to use for that experience.

This lens is the cumulative weight of all our previous experiences. As such, it occupies the lofty peak on our diagram. Every experience a student is currently having is subject to and colored by the experiences of their past (their lens), even as it changes or reinforces that lens.

We all use multiple lenses every day which we look through to interpret our daily experiences. We take in information from our senses and our processing only after being filtered through our lenses. That means that not only do we focus on some information more than others (senses), connect them (or not) with prior experiences (processes), but they are also viewed (and sometimes distorted) by the lens we chose to use.

For example, think about watching a political debate with someone with different political affiliations. You are at the same place, watching the same debate, hearing the same words, and yet you both have very different views of what was said.

These Mental Models are not "good" or "bad"; they just are. To live to our greatest potential requires us to be aware of the lenses we have. Peter Senge (1990) has said (one of my favorite quotes of all time), "[the] structures of which we are unaware hold us prisoner"; your mental model is one of these structures.

Our lenses in life ultimately reflect our deepest beliefs about the world, beliefs that are so deeply embedded in our lives they seem to be "common sense" (to us). They are the values we carry with us every day to every experience. It is how we perceive the world—what we value, what we care about, and how we think things work. Some common lenses involve:

Money—how much is enough, its purpose, its worth, and its overall significance. . .

Politics—Democratic, Republican, independent, what is the role of government, who has the power, what is the best use of power. . .

Religion—pros and cons of any belief system, what does it look like when enacted, how does it change our daily behaviors. . .

Family—what do different roles look like (daughter, son, husband, wife, father, mother, step-, etc.), how important is it. . .

Gender—what are the expectations for each gender, what about those who do not neatly fall into either category, how does it constrain/advantage me. . .

Race—what limits/advantages does it carry, what systems are in place, how others see me, what rules impact me. . .

And more (geography, birth order, socioeconomic status, language(s), etc.). This isn't an exhaustive list, just some of the more common ones.

Since our mental models are invisible to many of us, they act like a self-fulfilling prophecy—we see what we want to see and hear what we want to hear. If I think you are a horse's bottom end (my lens), everything you do will be viewed through that lens—unless I am aware of that lens and am willing to Re-consider that view. We need to be aware of the lenses we have so that we can choose to keep or change them when they don't meet our deepest or changing needs.

Changing our mental model is the most challenging kind of learning. Consider this: How often do people change their mind about politics, race, or religion? What are the things that you're not supposed to talk about at family gatherings?

Changing a mental model requires that you Re-consider your current experience, *and all of the experiences leading up to your understanding as well.* Only the most powerful experiences can change a person's lens in one fell swoop—near death experiences, having children, committing to a long-term relationship, loss of financial stability, and moving to very different place are all examples of this, and may lead people to Re-consider what really matters in their lives.

Barring giving our students near-death experiences (not recommended), we cannot make anyone "learn (change)" anything, especially their mental models. One positive approach to helping students address their mental models is through the lens of creativity and fun.

Intellectual "fun" means having the confidence and willingness to "play" with ideas. Play encourages us to experiment with different lenses without harm to ourselves or to our self-ego. It is *play*—imagining "how else" without being held accountable to actually do the change that matters.

One key idea when thinking about mental models is to help people become aware of their beliefs (through their dispositions) so they can *choose* to keep them, modify them or change them a little at a time.

Classroom Examples:

1. If you believed that there was only so much success in the world, then how might you view someone else winning an award?
2. Imagine being a strawberry farmer whose livelihood depends upon how many strawberries he/she sells. How might you as a farmer view insects and pesticides?

3. Tell that same story from the viewpoint of the villain.
4. Describe what the bouncing ball would look like on the moon.
5. What would that rhythm sound like if the only instruments were made from wood and rocks?

The lenses through which we view our experiences shape our reality. We also must realize that some experiences are more powerful in terms of learning than others.

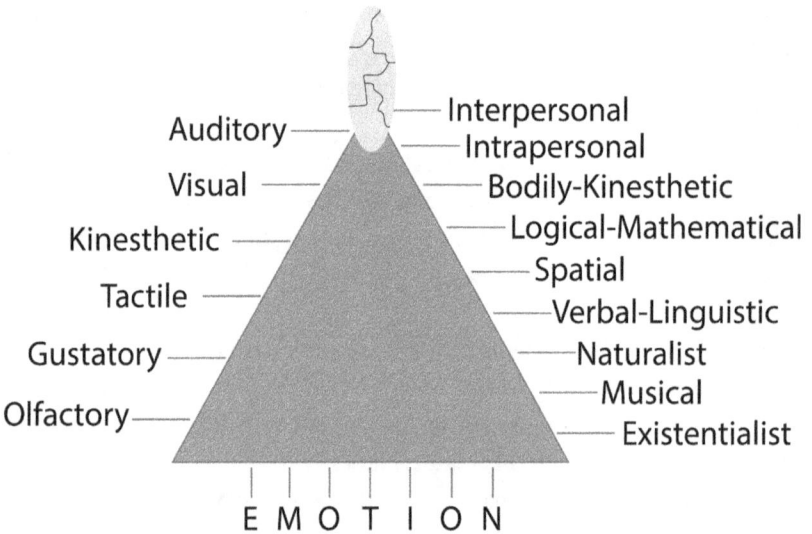

Diagram Explanation: The foundation for using experiences for learning rests upon the level of "emotion" of the experience. Things that are highly emotional (either good or bad) go right into our long-term memories.

Powerful experiences are not just about how many experiences you have had; they also include the notion of "How emotionally laden is the experience?" In our diagram, emotion is the foundation. I like to imagine that strongly emotional experiences have an intense color, and that less emotional experiences have less remarkable colors (deep red for a deeply angering experience, a pale red for mild irritation, transparent for neutral).

Imagine a box of marbles mostly filled with clear marbles. The clear marbles represent the mundane experiences that you may or may not remember, like driving to work or opening a door. Now imagine that there are several intensely colored marbles among the clear ones: These vibrantly colored marbles represent highly emotional experiences, the more emotional the experience, the more intense the color of the marble. Compared to the mundane clear marbles, the vibrant marbles stand out, just like how out of all the days I attended class I can remember that one time I called my second grade teacher "Mom" with perfect clarity.

Experiences with unusually strong emotional content go right into long-term memory, no matter what lens, sensory detail, or processes are associated with it. Emotion is the gatekeeper to long-term memory (think of your most embarrassing moment—no matter how long ago chances are your face still gets red, you start to sweat . . . the physiological body response of that emotion goes right along with your experience for years afterwards).

Strong emotions are frequently connected to: success, failure, embarrassment, achievement, recognition, belittlement, pride, getting caught doing something "wrong," errors, meeting goals, novelty, unexpectedness, surprise, cognitive dissonance (ideas that defy what people think they know), a-ha moments, and punishment, and can be either personal or social in nature.

In terms of positive, emotionally charged learning, success is the greatest motivator. Success on any task is the result of four components: 1) the task itself; 2) personal ability/aptitude for that task; 3) time, effort and resources allocated by the individual to the task; and 4) luck (time, day, teacher, classmates, etc.). The one component that students control is number three—time, effort and resources they commit to the learning task.

One reason we need to celebrate more (a strong emotion) is that recognizing learning success allows students to put that positive experience into long-term memory. Having experienced success before gives students "hope" that they can be successful again. The teacher can then use that prior experience to help students overcome doubt when success is questionable.

Making the standard for success so low that everyone is successful (participation awards) takes away the emotional benefit of "success." Success must be the result of achieving learning (change), not participation. The person him- or herself must see the task as emotionally weighted (not the giver).

One last note about using Emotion as a learning tool. Things that students see as "relevant" have the emotional component built in to the experience! Relevant topics matter to students because those ideas are developmental in nature, have a needs-orientation, answer their stressors and concerns, and when done well, answer their own questions (a-ha moments).

Classroom Examples:

1. What would it feel like to win that big award?
2. Imagine you discovered an energy source that changed the world. How might that change who you were?
3. How might you deal with losing a state championship game?
4. Describe a moment when persevering paid off for you.
5. Explain this statement: "The lows in my life allowed me to appreciate the successes I have had."

The experience triangle with senses, processes, mental models and emotion matters because:

1. The more observations you make (senses and processes), the more information you will have to "play" with and use for processing (thinking) later.
2. Learning to play with our mental models allows us to better understand ourselves and others (a key component of empathy).
3. Learning is an emotion-laden experience (change is risky business).
4. Our experiences are the basis for all our other thinking skills (we always go back to what we know and have experienced).

Sarah says to her classmates, "My person in the Rowlett Station skirmish was a black free-born midwife. I knew a little about the Civil War but hadn't really thought about all the people who'd been affected by those battles. It's making me reconsider what I think about wars and sending our troops off to battles."

8

INDUCTION AND THE NEED FOR MULTIPLE EXPERIENCES

Several weeks have gone by. Mr. James references the existing diagram all the time, and the students are beginning to think about and use the diagram for themselves, even outside of class.

Mr. James starts class today by putting students into groups. He puts Sarah, Jack, Rachel and Ramone into one group and gives the following prompt: "Define 'freedom.' Give three examples that match your group definition and three examples where you do not have 'freedom.'"

As they are working, Mr. James draws

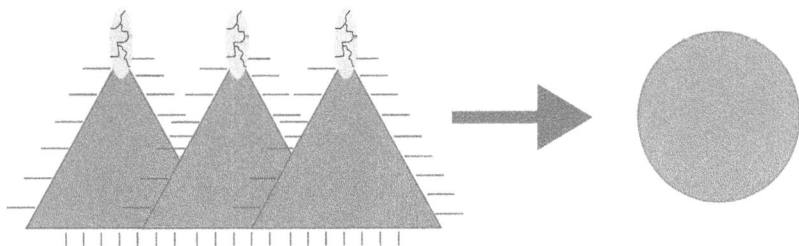

"Alright, everyone! I know you're working, I'll be quick: I just want to point out that I've added something to our diagram. So far, we've been talking about an experience—as in one experience, one run-in with the police, one job interview, one evening playing Dungeons and Dragons. One."

He points to the diagram. "Going on one interview does not make you an interview expert. One policeman does not represent all policemen. Right? The more experiences you have, and the more robust those experiences are, the better you can understand 'The Big Picture.'

"OK, you can continue working."

Experiences (the more robust and diverse the better) are the foundation for more complex thinking. Individuals create what they "know" based upon their experiences. A single experience is what you see, feel, taste, and hear (senses), understood through the way you tend to understand the world (interpersonal, logical, spatial, etc.), translated through your life lens (paradigm), and colored with emotions. We are our experiences (and how we think about them!).

But we have to break it down, because you are nothing but your experiences. There's a world of difference between knowing something intellectually (theoretically) and knowing something based upon hands-on (3-D) experiences. It's the difference between reading about ice skating and actually ice skating—not the same thing at all.

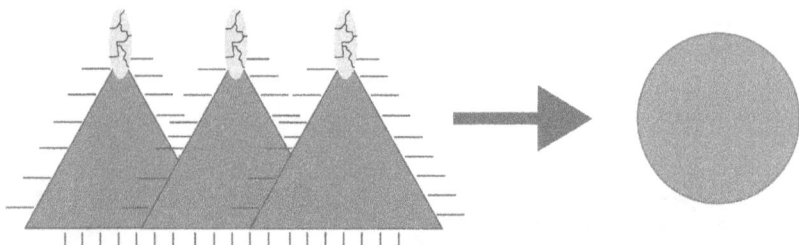

Diagram Explanation: The three triangles linked together represent Multiple Experiences (not just three) with any given thing. Those experiences include the senses, the multiple intelligences, the emotional context and the lenses that each individual has applied. Those multiple experiences allow the individual to create their own "conceptual understanding" (the circle) of whatever has been experienced. Change the experience(s) and you change the conceptual understanding by the individual.

Thinking Question Induction Cue Words:

Concept	Rule	Central concept
On the whole	Name	Generalization
*Label	Pattern	Idea
Formula	Big Idea	Principle
Definition		

* *Label* is another term for "word." Almost every label we apply (word we use) is the representation of our experiences with that idea. *Car, book, poem, racket, dinner, phone* and all the rest of the words we use are the representation of our many experiences with that thing. Our definitions of the words we use are always our personal definitions based upon our experiences.

The brain is an organ, and organs are defined as different tissues that work together to complete a particular function. The brain's function is to seek patterns. When we recognize a pattern we give that pattern a name and/ or label such as *dog, book, apple, friend, mom.* Basically all the words we use are representations of our experiences that our brains have tied together.

And since our perceptions are unique to us, everything we think we know is contextual (based upon our personal experiences). The interesting thing is that we find those patterns while living in a very messy world in terms of experiences (they are not sequential, nor linear—experiences happen when they happen).

Our brains are able to connect those experiences together and make "sense" of them. This "making sense"—finding the commonalities (the sticks our experiences have in common) among varied experiences—is called Inductive Reasoning. It is how we learn outside of classrooms. This is also why personal words and working definitions are so unique—they are based upon personal experiences (my conceptual understanding of the term *mom* is based upon my experiences with all the moms I have ever known, heavily weighted toward my own mom).

The making of generalizations (this word means this) looks like the following:

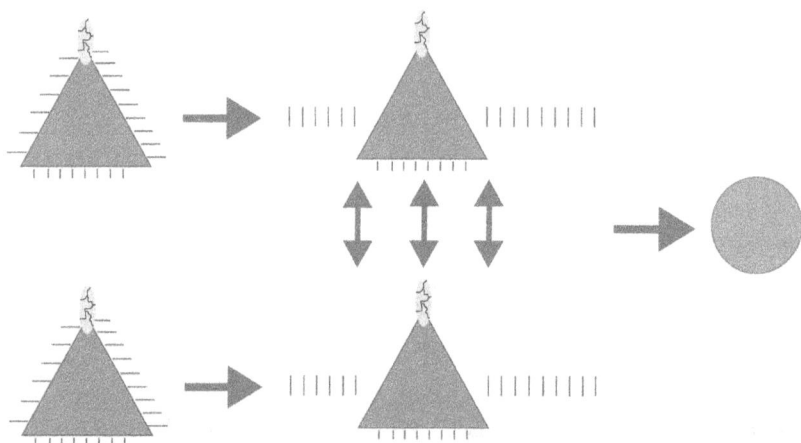

Diagram Explanation: For every experience (triangle) we have, we view that experience with our senses (sticks on the left), we process it in certain ways (sticks on the right), we view it through our mental models (lens) and we assign some emotional quotient to it (sticks on the bottom). When we have another (or more) experience with the same category of thing, we break apart our prior experience and look for "sticks" that are similar and different from each other—this is called Induction. Things that have similar sticks (a pattern) are assigned a "label."

This step of thinking is fundamental for teachers to understand. If there are no concrete experiences, any word or definition is memorized (theoretical) at best. A definition alone has no sticks of senses, no processes, no lenses and no emotional flavors. That means that the understanding has no depth and no complexity, and allows for little to no ownership of the understanding. The word is only a definition; it does not represent an accumulation of experiences.

POWER OF MULTIPLE EXPERIENCES

When it comes to truly understanding a concept (a term, a definition) it really does matter how many, how diverse, and how emotionally laden the experiences an individual has had with that concept.

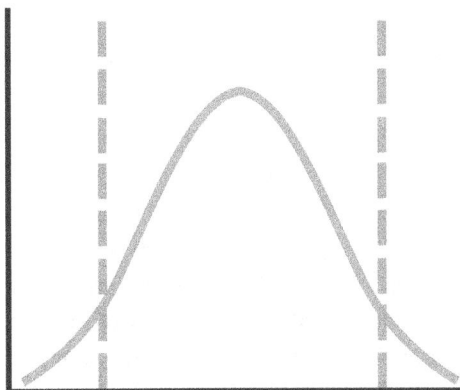

Diagram Explanation: The bell-shaped curve represents the variety in any experience—fishing, movies, dogs, apples, etc. Most are "normal" (somewhere in the middle of the curve) but there are always some that are especially wonderful (far right end) and some that are terrible (far left end). Generalizations mean knowing what is in the middle *and* that it is also appropriate (and still normal) to have examples at either end of the spectrum.

Individuals need enough (varied) experiences to know what is "normal" and accepted and what is unusual.

On the whole, generalizations allow us to talk about the bell-shaped curve of experiences (normal, unique, isolated, singular, common, etc.). There is always some variation in any kind of experience (fishing, listening to music, cooking/eating a meal, etc.) and it is important to know where that one specific experience falls among all the experiences.

Note: Generalizations are not stereotypes. Stereotypes are frequently stated as "All (of any thing) exhibit these characteristics or act the same." Stereotypes attempt to define any one idea as the same thing. Generalizations include the idea of variation with some commonalities.

The question becomes what is "normal variation" and what is so unusual as to be noticed. Learners need multiple, varied experiences to have a more complex understanding of what the experiences were all about.

Imagine for a moment that you live on a ranch in an isolated part of Montana (not hard to imagine if you've ever visited Montana). You're ten years old and your family raises black labs. That means you play with black labs, feed black labs, and sell black labs. Your world is filled with black labs.

And since you do not get off the ranch much, your definition of "dog" is almost the same as that of "black lab." So the first time you see a wiener dog, you might not even think "dog"—you are unsure of what that animal is, because to you (based upon your life experiences), dogs are black, weigh about 70 pounds, and act in goofy, lovable ways.

Multiple, diverse experiences with the same concept make thinking and working definitions more robust (and frustrating to define); yet deep understanding means to know what the norm is (what is a normal variation) and what is an outlier.

That means if I really wanted someone to create a robust definition of the concept "dog" (inductively) I would have to have them experience big dogs, little dogs, dogs with shaggy fur and dogs with almost none. I would provide old dogs and puppies, working dogs and lap dogs, purebred dogs and mutts. To truly "understand" the concept, the individual must have multiple perspectives on the same issue (the central concept in question).

This idea of making sense from multiple experience gets away from the idea of simplifying complex ideas and looking for one right answer. Providing multiple experiences allows students to create their own definitions and understandings, and that means students have a choice and can contribute to the group's understanding.

The more diverse the experiences, the more complex (and interesting) the thinking.

Complexity Alert: Concepts or generalizations can vary in size.

Big concepts are big circles—like "dogs"
Middle-sized concepts—middle-sized circles—hunting dogs, or herding dogs, or toy dogs
Small concepts—sub-concepts—little circles (exist within the big circle)—labs, poodles

It matters that you as the teacher know the concept and/or the sub-concept you are teaching, *and* make it explicit (all the small facts get connected to that label in your students' heads). If it is a sub-concept, connect it explicitly with the concept itself; this matters because it allows the teacher to scaffold teaching, broaden the concept over time and have students access what they already know at the beginning of any instructional unit.

Classroom Examples:

1. What concept do the strawberry, kiwi, and peach represent?
2. Generally speaking, after reading "The Three Little Pigs" and "The Wolf's Version of the Three Little Pigs" how does perspective change a story?

3. After interviewing five of the award winners, what common character-istics did you find?
4. Considering our experiences with all six simple machines, how might we define the term *work*?

Thinking Warning!

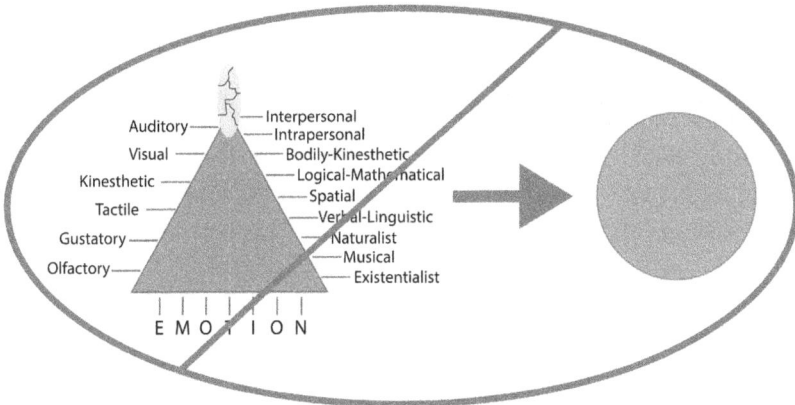

Diagram Explanation: One experience with anything leads to faulty conclusions (generalizations)—they become one and the same thing, fodder for stereotyping. If you want complex understanding from your students, you must give them multiple experiences with the same concept!

Too frequently in school, teachers provide one example (one experience) with a concept and study it for weeks, as if they were teaching a concept (a circle). The fact of the matter is they are teaching one experience (one triangle) and expecting students to generalize from that *one* experience, like studying only wiener dogs for an entire unit and then expecting students to understand the concept (and all the variations) of "dog."

Teaching only one experience as a concept is problematic in terms of thinking because:

1. It is tough to be creative when you have only experienced one thing (creativity is the ability to combine things that have not been com-bined before).

2. There is no sense of "normal" or where that one experience falls along the bell-shaped curve of experiences.
3. The "generalization" of the concept is so narrow (one experience only)—it's tough to transfer the learning to other concepts.
4. It is challenging for any one experience to be equally relevant to a classroom of students (because of who they are and what they currently care about).
5. Multiple, diverse experiences increase the chances of finding something more students might find relevant.

Thinking for yourself includes coming up with the rules, the definition, the concept, and pattern for yourself! Multiple, diverse experiences allows for students to "own" their own learning, which allows them to recall that information more easily and readily.

Rachel remarks, "But doesn't the idea that everyone has their own definition for the same thing really complicate life? I mean, I get that we all have different experiences, but there are right and wrong ideas and answers, aren't there?"

Mr. James: "I hesitate to give a short answer, Rachel. I might say, especially since we're in school and you're supposed to be learning, that there are 'More Correct' answers, and there are 'Less Correct' answers, which under some circumstances might be considered incorrect. When I'm given an 'incorrect' answer, I try to give you more information, or implore you to use a different skill to come up with a 'more correct' answer. Does that make sense? Thinking is messy: One person's correct answer is another person's incorrect answer."

THINKING IS MESSY

Circular Thinking and the Re-Concept

A week or so later, Mr. James is out of class; his kids are sick and he has to stay home and take care of them. There's a sub, but the class is working on group projects and planned what they'd be working on the day before.

After reading Mr. James' notes, the sub says, "Your instructor told me that you'd know what to do for the day, but asked me to add this to 'the class diagram.' Does anyone know what that means?"

Jack jumps up and reads the note over the sub's shoulder and adds this to the diagram:

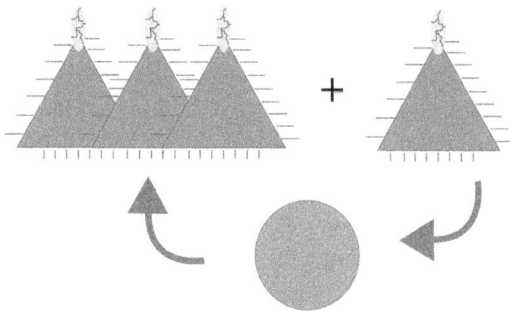

Diagram Explanation: Again, the triangles represent multiple (not just three) experiences and still include all the senses, processes, emotions, and mental models. We create our conceptual understandings from those experiences. Those understandings and experiences actually represent a dynamic relationship where we go back and forth between what we have experienced and what we think we know. This back and forth iteration is heightened when we add a new experience or new perspective to the mix.

We are all prisoners of our past experiences. We always come back to what we have experienced, what we think we "know" from our personal experiences—with our mental models in place and with our emotional baggage; we are not blank slates. And while the thinking diagrams attempt to make thinking look concrete and sequential, it just isn't that simple. Thinking is circular.

When we have an experience (either a new one or another of the same) we may Re-think what we know based upon the interplay between new and old experiences. In the face of new experiences we can:

1. Ignore the new experience,
2. Modify our current thoughts, beliefs or actions, or
3. Struggle to put a new belief system, knowledge or skills into place.

Which of those three options any person chooses has everything to do with the learning environment, the self-esteem of the learner, and his or her willingness to take learning risks.

Circular Thinking means that students will continually come back to the concrete experiences you provide *in relationship* to what they think they already know from their prior experiences (the triangles).

Here is an example of Circular Thinking for the concept of "dog." Imagine the life of a three-year-old. They do not have a "dog" of their own, but they have random experiences with dogs during the course of their everyday activities.

Even as a three-year-old, they have multiple experiences with "dogs." They see dogs in the streets, they get to pet them in the park, and one of their friends has one which they get to pet, smell, and play with. And the dogs they "see" are not the same: Some are big, some small, some yellow, some black. Yet their parents call them all the same: "doggy."

Sometimes as they are learning the concept "dog" they make mistakes—a cat is a dog, a squirrel is a dog, a raccoon is a dog, and a Chihuahua is a dog (oh wait a minute, it *is* a dog!). Almost anything that has fur, four legs, ears and a tail gets the same label.

For every experience they have with a "dog" (right or wrong) they have to put that experience with all their other experiences with that concept. And let's be very clear, it's a very fine line between dogs and cats (and squirrels and raccoons).

Thinking is a constant iteration of "what you think you know" in light of the new experience. That type of thinking takes place outside the school and in those real-life settings is considered "normal."

Sometimes the "new information" that a teacher provides is in the form of facts. Experiences are not necessarily facts. Facts are the summary or synthesis of multiple experiences. Facts are the "distillation" of multiple experiences. Many times facts are right (but they can be wrong too). Facts may also be: reliable, accurate, unbiased (or at least the bias is known) and many times measurable (or the result of those measurements).

Facts may also be statements by experts from the field. In those cases we give credence to the statement because the acknowledged expert has said something is so. Interestingly, even when facts are presented, they also fall along a bell-shaped curve of "accepted" or "normal" belief.

In all cases (either a new experience or the introduction of new facts) the learner has to compare those new thoughts to the experiences they themselves have had. They get to Re-think what they think they know in light of that new information. Thinking is hard work.

For teachers, it would be more structured to provide students with lots of different dogs and ask the following questions:

Sensory questions: What does each dog: Look like (visual)? Smell like (olfactory—both dry and wet)? Feel like (tactile)? How does it move (kinesthetic)? What do they sound like (auditory)? It may not be appropriate to ask them to Taste the dogs ☺ (although that does occasionally happen).

Processing questions (connect to what they already know): How and why do dogs interact with people (Interpersonal)? Why does petting a dog when you are sad make you feel better (Intrapersonal)? What role do dogs play in nature (Naturalist)? How are the barks of dogs like that of something else, like a coyote or wolf (Musical)? What stories might you have about a dog (Verbal-Linguistic)? Do dogs go to heaven (Existentialist)? What are dogs worth (Logical-Mathematical)? What pictures of dogs might you have seen or made, and are they correct or incorrect (Spatial)?

The more Sense and Process questions you ask, the more robust the experience (and the easier it is for them to Re-call that experience and the associated details).

CIRCULAR THINKING AND THE RE-CONCEPT

The Re-Concept emerged from many different words: Re-think, Re-view, Re-conceptualize, Re-call, Re-imagine, and Re-consider. It means to think once more about what you think you know in light of something new, some new experience, new perspective or new thought.

The Re-Concept acknowledges the fact that you already have something in your head (a conceptual understanding), and you are going to think about it *again* in light of something new (information, insight, experience, etc.). This is the essence of thinking.

The Re-Concept also means your current dispositions, thoughts and skills are placeholders for new personal growth. And that works if your definition of learning encompasses a change in thoughts, beliefs or actions.

For our students, by the time they are in schools, they already have thoughts, beliefs and actions in place (they are not blank slates for us to write upon). It also does not work to tell them their disposition, knowledge, or skill is wrong because what they are doing already appears to meet their needs (and match their experiences).

We have to *entice,* not force them to Re-think (habits of mind) what they already think they know—to *better* meet their needs. Providing a new and different experience (concrete is best) pushes them to think beyond their current experiences.

Re-thinking, re-imagining requires a "willingness" to consider something new (a disposition) and go back to what you think you know. *If* you have planned their experiences in powerful ways (lots of senses, processes and emotion), they can always access those experiences and Re-think them.

Powerful learning requires a safe environment to "wonder" and consider new experiences and new definitions/alternatives. Learners need enough facts and perspectives, an environment that reduces risk, and enough time to Re-consider how else to meet their needs. And even under ideal circumstances, learning—especially at the belief level—takes effort, resources, and time. Change is challenging.

We are each constrained and defined by our personal experiences. They are how we think and what we value. Providing multiple, complex experiences allows students to "think" for themselves, develop their personal conceptual understandings which explain *all* their experiences (including the ones you designed for them).

This book presents Thinking Questions in a linear format, but again, let's be clear: Thinking is not linear. When what we think we know, can do or believe is in doubt, we always go back to our experiences.

Jack, Sarah, Ramone and Rachel are sitting at their table chatting.

Jack begins: "Ya' know, I was down in Selma last year with my dad going to a Civil War reenactment. We drove down that street in Selma and it looked like any other street I have been on . . . stores, people walking, cars driving by. I would never have guessed that something so powerful had happened there."

Sarah responds, "Last year I acted in *To Kill a Mockingbird*. If I ever get the chance to act in that play again, I will totally play my role differently."

Ramone says, "Coach was talking the other day about knowing your adversary better than you know yourself if you really want to be successful. I think I am starting to see what he meant."

Rachel is struggling. She says, "I kind of see what Mr. James is trying to do. I am just not sure that it will help me do well on the AP exam or get into the college I really need to get into."

III

"PAST" THINKING QUESTIONS

Ramone, Rachel, Sarah and Jack are sitting around talking about things they do in their free time: Jack talks about last weekend when he got to go to a Civil War reenactment, how awesome it was, the time-period food he ate, the smells, the songs—the whole thing was incredible!

Sarah talks about her last play—she got to both act in the play and be the set designer. She got to make the play come alive, and entertain the audience as well!

Ramone talks about the football team and how winning on the last play was maybe the most exciting thing that ever happened in his life.

Rachel talks about the college her brother is attending and how important it is for her to live up to her family's expectations. She feels a lot of pressure to succeed.

Our experiences matter. They include our senses, how we process those experiences, the mental models we carry with us and the emotional highs and lows that color our worlds (and our memories).

And yet, we are more than just our experiences. John Dewey (1934) has said we do not learn from experiences; we learn from *processing* those experiences. Again, our definition of learning is a change in thoughts, beliefs, or actions. That means we frequently have the same experience over and over again, because nothing changes (which means we have not learned from those experiences).

Using our experiences (and those the teacher constructs for us) as our basis for "thinking" allows us to personalize our knowledge. Making our experiences Explicit allows us to share experiences and learn from others' experiences. We get to play with what we think we know!!

In this section we address thinking about our past experiences. Chapter 10 discusses Analysis, and chapters 11 and 12 deal with more specific types of analysis thinking with Same/Different and Insight Questions. Chapter 13 addresses Appraisal types of thinking, chapter 14 addresses Summary and finally chapter 15 models Evaluation. Each of these thinking skills requires the thinker to Re-examine their experiences and what they think they know.

10

ANALYSIS

Rachel and Jack are talking about the new *Star Wars* movie that's just come out. Rachel really liked it, but Jack thought that it was recycled and stale, but can't quite articulate why.

"Can I interject?" asks Mr. James. "I think this is a great way to get into today's lesson. OK, now I know that you've all seen your fair share of movies, so you have lots of experience to draw from. I want everyone to partner up and make a list for me: I want to know the parts or stages—however you interpret that—of a good, standard adventure movie."

Analysis is one of the most common Thinking Questions. Teachers frequently ask students to List things, Classify things, or write the Steps of things. Unfortunately, most of the time those ideas have already been lectured on and the task becomes a re-call/memorization task rather than a Thinking task. Analysis means going from the whole, the concept itself, to the parts that make it up—by yourself.

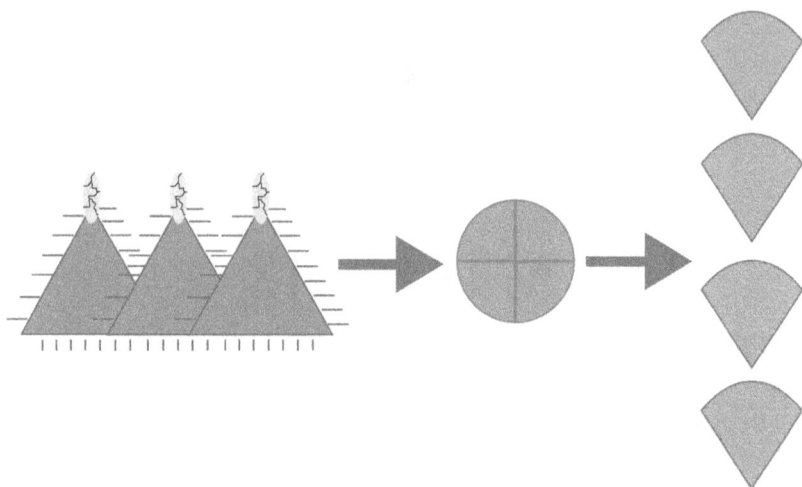

Diagram Explanation: Our conceptual understandings (the circle) emerge from our experiences (the triangles), and more importantly how we think about those experiences. When our understanding is robust, we can then think about those pie pieces that are common among ALL the experiences (not just one or a few). In the diagram there is nothing magical about four pie pieces other than they represent however many pieces of the whole the learner can identify.

Thinking Question Analysis Cue Words:

List	Parts
Steps	Classify
Sequence	Mind map
Pieces	Components
Elements	Common elements
Commonalities	Common characteristics

A robust analysis is based upon multiple experiences with a *concept*, not describing a single experience (that would be observation—senses, processes, mental models and emotions). That is why a diverse set of experiences creates a more thoughtful analysis that addresses the norms of the concept being studied.

Analysis in this context is more challenging than we might think. For example, consider the following question: "What precursors led to the Civil

War?" Many think that it is an analysis question. Since it only asks about one experience (the Civil War), in reality that question is an Observation-Process question. An analysis question would be: "What common characteristics are there between the precursors to all wars?" (or at least the Civil War and one or two other wars).

Analysis is really the process of making explicit "which sticks (senses and processes) are shared among the many experiences." Do they all look the same? Feel the same? Share the same pattern? Exhibit similar causes and effects? Analysis says that for this concept, all (or at least generally speaking) the examples share these same features.

For example, if the concept under study was "bicycles" and we had studied (experienced) road bikes, mountain bikes, cruiser bikes and racing bikes, we could say (analysis) bicycles have: two wheels, handlebars, pedals (two), chains, and so on. If we had studied different types of bicycles than the ones we did (different experiences), our analysis might be different.

To teach analysis thinking successfully requires that the teacher know those 3-D experiences very well, and constantly reference those experiences when analysis items are incorrect (What about our experience with X?—rather than "Wrong.") This continuous connecting of thinking to prior experiences and prior types of thinking is the "art of teaching thinking."

For powerful learning to take place the learner must come up with the pieces by themselves. The teacher's role is to make sure their pieces match all the experiences that have been provided. Student answers are then not right or wrong; instead they become the basis for asking "What about (a certain specified experience they have had that adds more information)?"— thus requiring students to "think" for themselves, to Re-consider their own answers with more information, and to account for all their prior thinking and experiences.

Multiple, powerful (in terms of remembering) experiences are key to a good analysis. The teacher's role becomes one of leading students to "discover" the pieces for themselves, based upon the concrete experiences that have been provided. One cannot "assume" students have had specific prior experiences because some will not have had those experiences, and that impacts their ability to find those important pieces.

With circular thinking the sticks of experience (senses and processes)

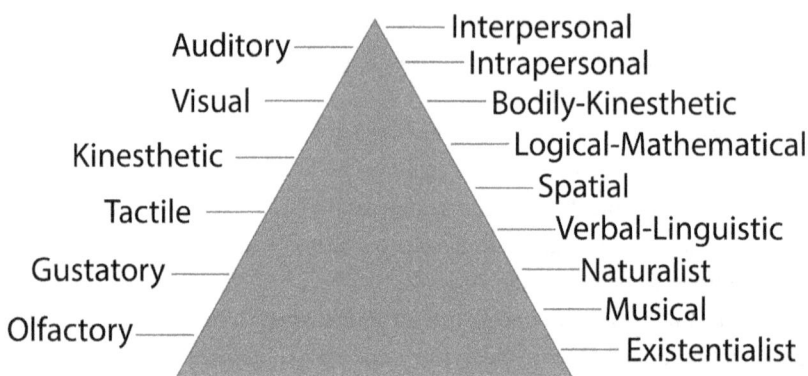

become more and more helpful to good analysis because they provide concrete data for students to consider. They can ask themselves, "Is it true for the entire concept or just one experience?" They can begin to grapple with where that example falls along the bell-shaped curve of "normal."

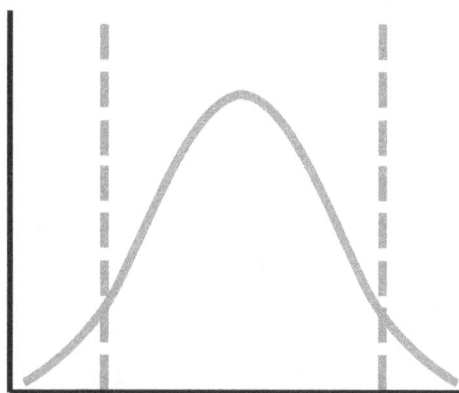

Sometimes of course students do not identify the pieces of a concept correctly. When that happens (and it will) the teacher's fallback position is to go back and add more concrete experiences so that the pieces misidentified become more obvious. Again, students must come up with the answers for themselves (if they are in fact Thinking Questions).

To use Thinking Questions well, you have to be clear about the concept you mean to teach, and then provide experiences that match the concept. Maybe you focused on a sub-concept (terriers) rather than the concept you intended (dogs). By limiting the experiences you narrow the analysis.

Another common error (perhaps the most common) is having students memorize the parts of a concept and thinking they are "doing" analysis. It might sound like: "List the parts of the cell," or "List the 50 state capitals." For analysis to be "thinking" on the part of the students *they* must come up with the pieces on their own (continuously referencing their concrete experiences).

Forcing students to memorize lists limits the sorts of experiences they can bring to bear on a question. There are multiple correct answers for an analysis question, and students will give different answers depending on who they are.

There is a Cost for having students think for themselves: You will cover less material (and it is difficult to provide and think of concrete experiences for all concepts). The Benefit is they remember experiences (and can access them), they figure stuff out for themselves and they grow the ability and confidence to think for themselves. Thinking allows students to create new habits of mind, and by empowering our students we make ourselves dispensable. That just takes more time.

Analysis also matters as a foundational piece of future thinking as well. One characteristic of creativity is "putting pieces together that have not been combined before." That means that being aware of the pieces (analysis) from multiple concepts provides opportunities to be creative.

The pieces matter when it comes to thinking. The process of Analysis Thinking is both the forest (the concept—the circle) and the trees (the pie pieces) (and the shrubs and the animals and the soil, etc.). Thoughtful analysis is really iterative; it is about the relationships between the pieces and whole. The concept itself is more than just the pieces; it is the pieces and how those pieces are related.

Classroom Examples: (Thinking task for the reader—What experiences would have been provided so that students could answer the following analysis questions? See appendix A.)

1. List the parts of a fruit.
2. Create a story map for journeys.

3. What commonalities are there between people identified as "explorers"?
4. What do these four "invasion games" have in common?

Ramone is talking with Mr. James after class. "You know, Mr. James, you're really messing me up. Last night I was thinking about all the different types of games I've played: soccer, tennis, football, and Ping-Pong. I got to thinking about how each one had their own set of rules (but that they all had rules), had a specific field of play and a specific way of scoring points and winning. That's analysis right?"

Mr. James responds, "Yes, it is, Ramone. Kind of fun to actually figure stuff out on your own, isn't it?"

11

ANALYSIS CONTINUED

Same/Different

Mr. James walks into the room to hear Sarah ask Jack, "So what is the difference between the soldiers who fought in the Civil War and those who fought in WWI?"

Sometimes comparing two closely related things helps you remember certain characteristics of each more fully. In other words, as you think about one concept, you remember characteristics of another concept. Your "analysis" of each is enhanced by comparison of the two.

"Well," says Jack, "I think that the biggest difference would be technology. They didn't have machine guns or airplanes or really effective artillery until early 1900s I think. Technology made it possible to kill multiple hundreds, or even multiple thousands of people in just one battle, which would have been unthinkable during the Civil War. That's a pretty big change."

This process of analyzing two closely related ideas is called "same/different." It involves developing the pieces (analysis) of two separate concepts (closely related) and then comparing the items on each list. Same/different thinking provides opportunities for students to develop more sophisticated analysis of each concept.

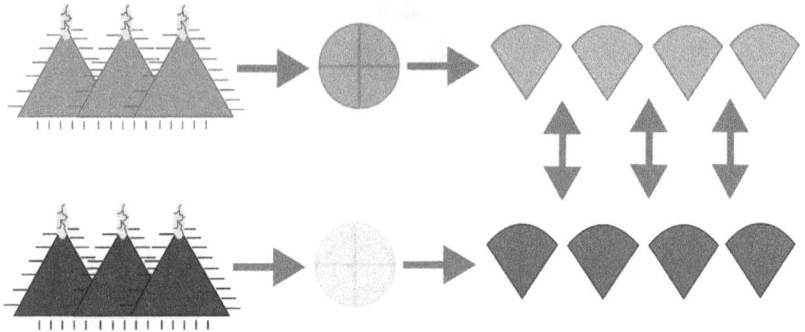

CHAPTER 11

Diagram Explanation: This thinking skill begins with completing two separate Analysis activities. After those Analyses (the pie pieces) are complete, then comparing the lists of "pieces" (the arrows) begins. That comparison is what we call Same/Different.

Thinking Question Same/Different Cue Words*:

Same	Different
Alike	Dissimilar
Similar	Compare
Contrast	Differentiate

* *Note:* In terms of thinking, Same/Different is exactly the same process as Induction, the difference being Same/Different compares concepts (instead of experiences).

To do Same/Different well requires that students first develop each analysis list individually, *then* compare the two lists—being allowed to add ideas to each separate list. The key point of same/different is to create a better, more thoughtful, and more accurate Analysis. It allows the learner to add more pieces to each analysis list, which allows for a more detailed picture of the whole (the concept in question).

Analysis matters because those are the pieces that are shared by *all* the examples of that concept. The lists are specific to the concept, and only that concept. So while there are many similarities between dogs and cats, the analysis same/different lists *need* to show how they are different (things on one list but not on the other).

Specificity matters. Since we all have our own "working" definitions for almost any term, clarity requires that we both have the same conceptual understanding of the term we are both using. Your idea of "good" may be totally different than mine, and yet when we talk and say the word *good*, we both nod, thinking we understand that other person.

All analysis thinking requires the learner to "Circular think," first going back to the experiences themselves, then the concept itself, and then the pieces of the concept. Analysis requires the intrapersonal question "Is it true for the concept or just the experience?" Remember, Same/Different is for conceptual understanding, NOT the experiences themselves.

Classroom Examples:

1. Compare fruits and vegetables.
2. Differentiate between success and failure.
3. Compare plot and setting.
4. Contrast states' rights versus federal rights.

Jack continues, "But, you know, everyone was still trying to fight the war according to the modern world's rules—so I guess that makes the two conflicts pretty similar except for the technology thing."

12

INSIGHT

Mr. James listens to Jack's reasoning, and asks a question of his own: "Nice work with the same/difference analysis, Jack. Do you see any similarities between your typical WWI narrative and the recent lectures we've had about bullying?"

Sometimes comparing two wildly different things helps you connect things not usually connected and see very deep patterns and/or similarities. In other words, as you try to find similarities and differences between two very different ideas, sometimes you come across similarities that you have not noticed before. Your "analysis" of each is enhanced by comparison of the two (pieces that are invisible are not explicit).

"Um," says Jack. "Maybe. Give me a minute to think about it."

Sarah says, "Well, the speakers were sort of like generals planning an attack—maybe?"

Mr. James scratches his head. "Interesting comparison. I've never thought of it that way. I don't think you're wrong. Let me think about that."

This process of analyzing two wildly different ideas is called "insight." It involves developing the pieces (analysis) of two separate ideas (wildly different) and then comparing the items on each list. Insight thinking provides for opportunities to develop a very sophisticated analysis of each concept—and maybe find similarities that had not previously been noticed.

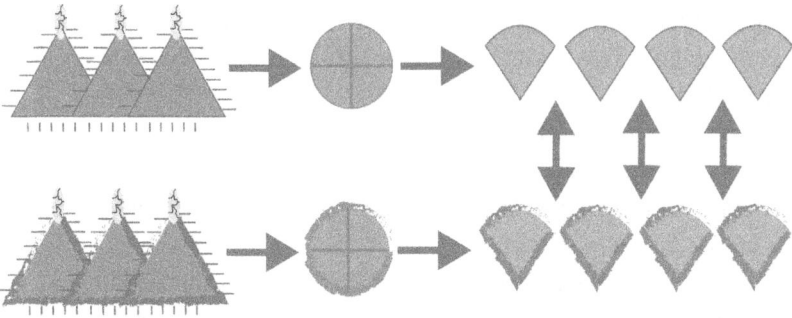

Diagram Explanation: Same exact thinking process as Induction and Same/Different—except the pie pieces (analysis) of the two concepts (the circles) being compared (the arrows) are vastly different (in your mind)—thus the squiggly lines!!

Thinking Question Insight Cue Words:

Connections	Inference
Insight	Patterns
Parallel pattern	Overlapping patterns
Interrelationships	Compare (very dissimilar things!)

So while comparing dogs and cats would be a Same/Different thinking activity, comparing dogs and computers, or dogs and skateboarding, or dogs and dictators would be an insight task.

Thinking note: The person asking the question determines if it is an insight or Same/Different question (not the person answering). And in the big scheme of things, the classification of the question is less important than the thinking process itself.

Frequently Insight has an emotional response, called "gestalt" or the a-ha! moment. When the person sees the connections or the pieces finally fall into place, they literally "feel" the answer! One other nonverbal sign of an insight question is when asked for the comparison, the person answering the question gives a big eye blink or at least a big furrow appears between their eyes. Those are some ways you know they are thinking!

CHAPTER 12

For many public school students (who have not been asked to "think" much before), they need to be pushed into comparing dissimilar things. After a short while, they will start making those connections themselves (especially to what they know well—fishing, games, music, etc.). They will say things like "This is a lot like skateboarding . . ." or "This reminds me of *World of Warcraft* . . ."

Again, the thinking for Insight is comparing things *not* closely related, even though the thinking process is the same as Same/Different. The idea is to look for deep patterns and previously unnoticed connections between things not normally compared.

Insight is a very high-order thinking skill. It requires the ability to connect things (deep patterns) with things not normally compared. It truly demonstrates a "depth of understanding" between multiple concepts.

To teach insight well, you have to teach the diagram—making the thinking both Explicit and Intentional. First provide experiences that support one concept and then experiences that support the other concept, and then compare.

Circular thinking: You may have to find out what they think they already know well (games, hobbies, crafts, learning process itself, etc.)—and then compare those things to the concept you are teaching.

Insight matters because recognizing connections (similarities and differences) simplifies our lives. Things that we previously thought were isolated become connected. The deep patterns become evident or the pieces of the concept suddenly become related when compared to some other concept.

In terms of classroom thinking, insight is a teacher's best friend. Again, insight is the analysis process of comparing two very different concepts (for the learner). That means comparing content to something the student knows well allows them to connect what appears (to them) to be very different concepts. This allows students to use what they already know to better understand a content concept—and maybe help make content more relevant.

For example, comparing the beginnings of a war to arguments with a friend, or rap lyrics to classical poetry, or trying a new trick to experimentation, or learning a new soccer move to movement concepts. At the deepest level, the central concepts we try to teach are always connected to everyday learning—just with different content.

Classroom Examples:

1. What connections are there between fruits and computers?
2. What common pattern exists between the ideas of plot and our interviews with people who have been recognized for their successes?
3. Identify the interrelationships between state rights and scoring at the X Games.

Sarah and Jack are still chatting when Jack asks, "So what do you think was the number one reason for WWI?"

13

APPRAISAL

Mr. James and Rachel are talking about the importance of grades. During their dialogue they talk about grades and what they might mean. They consider: measure of achievement, checkpoint for fact acquisition, work ethic, knowledge or skill evaluation. After a pause, Mr. James asks, "Those are all good reasons to grade; which one do you think is the most important?"

Appraisal is the intellectual act of assigning value to the pieces of the concept. It forces the person to make choices, identify the hierarchy, or rank the pieces in terms of importance. Not all pieces of almost anything are of equal value.

Wiggins and McTighe (1998) appraise (rank) content information in terms of "enduring, important, and familiar with" rankings. They posit that some ideas in any content area are enduring—they are the "big ideas" of the field, and other information is important—and thus worth knowing. Other ideas are not so critical to know—but might be nice to know depending on the situation.

Appraisal matters because we can't have or do everything we want. We have to pick and choose. It is the picking and choosing that makes the task complex, because our past experiences and our knowledge (at that time and place) have a dramatic impact upon how we rank order any list.

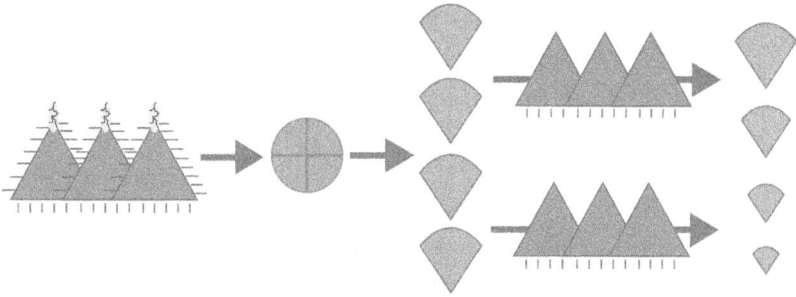

Diagram Explanation: After identifying the pieces (analysis), the learner then revisits their experiences and gives value to each of the pieces (different size pie pieces). Some things are always more important than other things (bigger pie pieces), and sometimes they really do not matter that much (the smaller pie pieces). Appraisal makes those rankings explicit, which then tells everyone else how they have experienced that concept.

Thinking Question Appraisal Cue Words:

Weigh	Rank
Rate	Grade
Prioritize	Most to least
Value	Least to most
One a scale of . . .	

Appraisal thinking is grounded in personal experiences (the triangles again). In terms of giving value to the items, criteria are mostly personal (versus professional) in nature. That means I will rank the items based upon my personal experiences—these things are most or least important to me based upon my prior experiences.

The thinking aspect of appraisal is not so much the right or wrong order of the ranking; the real thinking task is making explicit the "rationale" for ranking the items the way you did. The rationale connects directly to the prior experiences students have had with the concept, shows their knowledge (or lack thereof) about the concept and also makes explicit what the individual values. That is powerful information in just one thinking skill—and why it's a four-step thinking task.

CHAPTER 13

Rachel responds: "I think the most important reason for teachers to give grades is to help students get into the college of their choice, and then maybe to help rank students so that the smartest ones get some scholarships. It's a way for society to put money where it can be used wisely."

Another interesting aspect of Appraisal is that the rankings change with the context or a change in purpose. Ultimately, if you change the context or the purpose you change the rankings. And sometimes if you add more information you change the rankings as well.

Consider camping. Camping is a very contextual activity. There's car camping, beach camping, wilderness camping, boat camping, and more. In most cases of camping, space is a limiting factor—so the individual must prioritize the items they wish to take.

Car camping: Yes, take that music system! Wilderness camping: Better pack that water filter. Where (and how long) the camping trip is supposed to go totally changes the rankings of things to take—context matters. It reminds me of that saying: "You can have anything you want, but you can't have everything you want."

We are constantly appraising things: what to do, what to buy, where to give our time, effort and resources over a multitude of other choices—because our resources (or time or effort) are limited. Choice theory (Glasser, 1998) talks about how we control our actions to best meet our needs (versus whim, serendipity, luck, fate, etc.). The more thoughtful the experiences we have, the better (in meeting our needs) our rankings will be.

Another name for "thoughtful experience" could be called Reflection. It is the idea of Re-considering what happened, why it might have happened, and how to Re-create or avoid the same result the next time. In this light, reflection has a large "appraisal" component to it (this part went well, change this part the next time).

Sometimes as a novice, one emotionally laden experience will bias our entire conceptual understanding over all other experiences (no bell-shaped curve of understanding). The one experience was a total win (fantastic!), or alternatively a total loss (horrible). In either case that one experience overshadows other more "normal" experiences. The one experience becomes the conceptual understanding in spite of overwhelming evidence (other, multiple experiences) to the contrary.

When students are asked to provide their rationale for their rankings they provide the teacher (and the other students) with their personal experiences and knowledge of the concept at hand. They share what they have done, how they think about that experience and what they consider to be important and valuable. This is powerful information for any teacher who teaches people (rather than content).

Personal experiences are not "good" nor "bad"—they just are. This is especially true when you include the idea of Mental Models and how they influence a person's experiences. All the teacher can do to help individuals Re-prioritize is: 1) add more experiences (and more senses and processes), 2) have others share their experiences (build a stronger bell-shaped curve), and 3) show other ways of ranking with other rationale (in a safe learning environment).

Classroom Examples:

1. Prioritize the list of things you have to accomplish today.
2. Rank order the top three most important characteristics of a friend.
3. Rank the most important aspects that compose high-quality literature.
4. List your top five favorite foods from most to least favorite.
5. List your top five reasons for the causes of interpersonal conflict. Score each of them on a scale from 1 to 10 (ten highest).

Mr. James listens to Rachel's appraisal, and asks, "You know, I hang out with some admissions counselors; they're starting to notice that colleges are looking more at your extracurricular activities and letters of recommendation than your grades. Lots of colleges and universities don't even require an ACT or SAT score; does that change your appraisal at all?"

14

SUMMARY

Ramone and Mr. James have an ongoing trash-talking conversation about how interesting football is compared to the Civil War. They good-naturedly tease each other and try to convert the other to admit to liking their interest area more.

Today Mr. James tells Ramone, "I'll give you one more shot, Ramone—your last opportunity to save me from my own irrelevance: Convince me that football is worth playing using seven or fewer words. If you can do that, I'll paint my face for Friday's game."

Ramone says: "No body paint, no deal."

Mr. James: "OK. But if you can't convince me, you have to memorize and recite part of the Gettysburg Address and deliver it as a motivational pre-game speech to your teammates. Deal?"

"You're on."

Mr. James smiles and says, "I hope you have seven awesome words lined up."

A good summary is short, provides a clear mental picture of the concept, identifies the main point(s) and is grounded in experience. It is ultimately the "essence" of the concept.

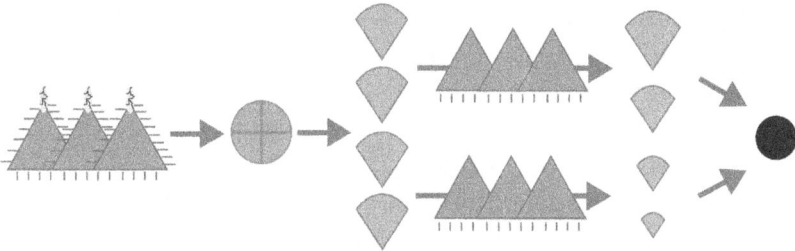

Diagram Explanation: Summaries are the small circles—smaller than the concept itself. They represent the "essence" of any concept (the big circle). Going through all the other thinking steps explicitly allows the learner to explicitly focus on the summary rather than all the pieces.

Thinking Question Summary Cue Words:

Main point	Main idea
Essence	Focal point
Sum up	In a nutshell
The bottom line	Reduce

Some summaries are more content focused and have little personal value added. One example might be the Bible verse John 3:16; for many individuals it is the entire Christian religion in one sentence.

Many times summaries also include the "emotion-laden" part of the experience—how the summarizer connects emotionally with the concept being summarized. The "summarizer" condenses their experiences, their own mental models and their emotion-laden experiences and uses analysis and appraisal skills to reduce the concept to what they believe to be most important.

Summaries are not the same as the number one most important item. They "summarize" the entire concept into a few words or a phrase (dog: man's best friend). They are that person's essence of the concept—not just the one part that is most important (appraisal). It is the result of analysis and appraisal in terms of thinking skills, and yet summaries are more complex than either.

That means that a person's summary tells everyone else how they really think about the concept at hand: their experiences, the emotions involved, the parts of that experience (analysis) and how those pieces are ranked (appraisal). That means summaries are Big Bang for the buck in terms of how that person is "thinking" (insight into a student's life)!

In a classroom setting, for the same Thinking Question prompt, there are always many summaries (all correct). It works that way because for any concept you are considering, there are many different experiences, mental models, and emotions. That means that the summaries of the students will be vastly different—which makes it very interesting and learningful.

For example, one summary of "dog" is "man's best friend." But that summary only applies to individuals who have multiple positive experiences with dogs. It would not be true of people who are frightened of dogs, been bitten by a dog, or are allergic to dogs. "Man's best friend" tells everyone not just about dogs but also about that person's experiences with dogs over time.

Ramone raises his hand partway through class and says: "Football is the human experience."

As a Thinking Question, teaching summary means knowing the differences between a Poor and a Good summary.

Poor Summary:	Good summary:
Too much information	Short and to the point
Too many main points	Main point(s) included
Poor analysis	Solid analysis provided when asked to elaborate
Poor appraisal	Complete appraisal provided when asked
Incomplete concept synthesis	Complete in relation to concept itself

Going through the other Thinking Questions first helps students:

Synthesize their many experiences,
Place those experiences in the bell-shaped curve of conceptual understanding,
Identify the pieces with detail and accuracy,

Rank the pieces in ways beyond only their experiences,
Synthesize knowledge about the concept, and
Synthesize their personal emotional values about the concept itself.

Classroom Examples:

1. What is the main point of fruit?
2. Summarize the concept of plot in seven words or less.
3. What is the focal point of the giving of awards?
4. In a nutshell, what can you say about your experiences with power?
5. Sum up the idea of decision making.

Ramone and Sarah are talking in the school lobby. Ramone asks, "I've really been thinking hard about this, and I want to know what you think: Do you really think I can get a football scholarship?"

Sarah: "I mean, I think you're good enough, but I'm not really a football expert. Have you already asked your coaches? They'd have a better idea than I would."

⑮

EVALUATION

Sarah and Rachel are talking about the school play they attended last night; it was the musical *Grease*. Rachel said she really liked the performance, the actors had high energy and they made her laugh. She thought it was really well done and gave it "two thumbs up."

Sarah, on the other hand, had a very different idea of what happened. She talked about how many of the actors missed their cues, their staging was off and some of the actors messed up their lines. She also liked their enthusiasm and they gave the audience everything they had—it was good entertainment. She gave the play a grade of C+.

While everyone might have and be entitled to their opinion, evaluations are a different type of thinking altogether.

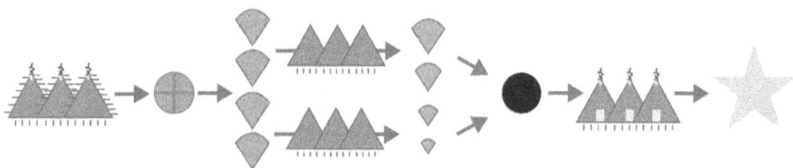

Diagram Explanation: Experts know the appropriate criteria (the boxes) for the situation and novices do not. Experts apply their professional lens of life when making evaluations (the lens on the top). A good evaluation includes the criteria being used *and* how they were applied to the situation.

Thinking Question Evaluation Cue Words:

Evaluate	Critique
Decide	Judge
Viewpoint	Identify the criteria you used to . . .
Belief	Establish quality of . . .
How might experts in the field . . .	

Differences between a poor and a good evaluation include:

Poor Evaluation:	Good Evaluation:
One point of view	Able to change perspective/criteria
May judge something unimportant	Based upon analysis, appraisal, summary
Based only upon personal experiences	Strengths and weaknesses identified
Biased	More objective (more than personal experiences)
Off the cuff	Fact based
Novice criteria used	Expert criteria used

Everyone does indeed have a right to their own opinion. However, that one person's opinion is not the same as an expert's evaluation (not even close). A more holistic graphic might be to imagine a continuum with Opinion at one end and Evaluation at the opposite. Consider global warming: Does the opinion of some politician hold the same weight as an environmental scientist?

To "evaluate" is to determine the value of or judge the quality of something. Evaluations determine the significance or worth of the thing in question by careful appraisal and study, and include making criteria in use explicit. Evaluation is a question of Quality (think *Zen and the Art of Motorcycle Maintenance*).

Great teachers are constantly evaluating the teaching and learning that takes place in their classrooms. Great teachers collect and use student learning data to help them judge the quality of learning taking place (versus only opinion as in "I think it went well"). As a teaching expert, they know the skills and strategies that determine high-quality instruction and where others might give a lesson a ten, they might give the exact same lesson a seven. The best teachers are also the most realistic about which lessons worked and which did not.

Criteria may also be called "deciders": the things you consider when making choices. For example, when I am at the grocery store I might consider the upcoming menu to help me "decide" what to purchase, how many people will be home might help me decide quantity, and also what is on sale (money is almost always a criteria for purchases).

Thinking becomes more complex when an individual has to judge the quality of a thing. We might have many experiences with that thing or idea, but have never thoughtfully considered what makes something "better" (of higher quality) than something else. So I might have an opinion (based upon my experiences)—but not an evaluation (based upon the "expert-level" criteria). An expert in the field knows the accepted criteria; a novice does not.

Mickey's Story: I have lived in houses for most of my life. Yet shopping and buying a new house is a nerve-wracking experience.

A few years ago my wife and I were looking for a new (to us) house on the river near our home—we've always wanted to live on the water. We found one that interested us and were about to start shopping for loans. As part of that process we also contacted a realtor friend about selling our current house. He mentioned that he would be happy to "walk through" the house we were considering buying. So we took him up on his offer.

It was like walking through an entirely different house. Since he was an "expert" he considered things we weren't even aware of: floodplain insurance, age of the septic system, building codes on the water, the age of the electrical wiring—the list was quite extensive.

He provided us with his evaluation as an expert—we on the other hand were looking at the house with our opinions in play.

In reality, as far as Thinking Questions go, Evaluation is really a two-part process:

1. Determining the expert criteria for the situation at hand, and
2. Applying those criteria to determine the quality of the thing in question.

A tricky part of "expertness" is that the criteria are very, very context specific. The process of using criteria can be generalized; the criteria themselves are context specific. That means that the criteria for determining the quality of, say, a flute, are very different than the criteria for determining the quality of, say, a bicycle. The process for finding the expert criteria are similar—find an expert and ask them!

All this matters because the focus on thinking Evaluation for students is for them to determine the expert criteria in use, in an inductive way. That means they need to look for, search and determine the criteria themselves, and then apply them. This thinking process includes concrete experiences, inductive thinking, analysis, appraisal, and summary thinking.

Classroom Examples:

1. Using what we have learned about powerful stories, identify your criteria and use them to critique this story.
2. Evaluate the farmer's use of pesticides.
3. Evaluate the musician's performance of this rhythm.
4. How might an actual scientist evaluate these results?

When we ask students to "think," we need to be aware of all the types of thinking that are required to answer that question. Concept? They need experiences. Analysis? They need conceptual understanding. Evaluation? They need all the other steps listed so far. And more importantly, they need to know Explicitly, how they have already thought.

"Explicit" and "Intentional" are crucial aspects to consider when teaching the art of thinking.

IV

FUTURE THINKING QUESTIONS

Mr. James walks into class today with a tennis ball, a Nerf basket that he hangs on the door, and a pirate hat. He looks at the class and gives the following prompt: "Using these three items, create a mini-play about the meeting of General Lee and President Lincoln. You have 30 minutes and it must include at least ten historically accurate facts. Think about this as a warm-up and practice round for our Meeting of the Minds project in the coming weeks. Feel free to be experimental, be silly, be whatever you want—except boring. You may begin."

Concrete, three-dimensional experiences are the foundation for our personal learning (at least until we are in our early 20s). More than that, *how* we think about those experiences (analysis, appraisal, summary, and evaluation) determines what we "learn" from any experience.

Sometimes we have experiences but don't think about them in powerful (thinking) ways or those experiences are not valued as important and powerful; therefore learning opportunities are missed or ignored. Those missed or ignored opportunities limit what we know, how we think, how we view reality—and what we ultimately can DO with those experiences.

PART IV

A quick Re-view before we move on. For students to "think" for themselves:

1. Start with multiple, concrete (3-D) experiences of the same concept. Include senses and processes, address mental models and emotional variables.
2. Define the concept that matches the experiences you provided. Remember the bell-shaped curve of experiences ("normal" versus exceptional).
3. Analyze the *concept* (not just one experience). Identify the pieces, and then compare them to closely related (Same/Different) and very different (Insight) concepts.
4. Appraise the pieces—give them value—using both prior experiences and set criteria.
5. Summarize the concept (key point, find the essence).
6. Evaluate—determine the criteria by which quality will be determined. Think like an expert!

Part IV deals with getting ready and DOing something with our learning—it is an Action-Orientation. It extends our thinking from what is to what might be.

We demonstrate our learning through our actions! That means we personalize the content, work through the thinking processes and then demonstrate our personal learning to others.

The last three steps are really the culmination of "thinking"—the end-in-mind we seek. If we Intentionally and Explicitly ask students to "think" for themselves, then we might hope to: 1) create self-actualized participants in a democratic society; 2) have students know themselves (strengths and weaknesses); 3) create an action-oriented habit of mind; 4) learn to work with the resources you have (not the ones you wish you had); 5) have students own their own learning (consciously and explicitly); and 6) make decisions like an expert.

Those end-in-minds require that we give students choices, power, and opportunities to fail (and succeed greatly). The answers they must seek are not the ones in textbooks—they are the answers that matter to them, today, right at this moment in time.

The next set of future Thinking Questions begins in chapter 16, a creativity focus. Chapter 17 focuses on critical thinking and finally chapter 18 includes both the planning and the actions that allow students to demonstrate their learning.

Mr. James looks around at the students as they work on the project: It's been 15 minutes, and it looks like Rachel, Sarah, Jack, and Ramone have decided that the Lincoln/General Lee meeting might have looked like a one-on-one basketball game: Sarah and Rachel are improv'ing a play-by-play as Ramone (Lee) and Jack (Lincoln) stage the game.

Mr. James smiles: "15 more minutes to get everything performance ready. Remember to include your ten facts in the show."

16

CREATIVITY

It's a Friday afternoon and finals are next week. The students feel fine for this class; they've effectively managed their time and feel good about both the test and paper written from the first-person perspective of someone who might have witnessed a Civil War battle. The conversations with Mr. James throughout the semester have helped to get them on board with the way he does things, so much so that they're beginning to get frustrated with their other classes and ask obnoxious questions of their other teachers like "Why do we have to know this?" and "What does X have in common with Y?"

Mr. James reins them in for a moment and gives them today's task: "Today I need you to begin thinking about your Meeting-of-the-Mind Role Plays (see appendix B) you will be doing next week. Using the personas you have developed, please list 75 Civil War events where those characters might interact."

A single, agreed-upon definition for "creativity" is hard to come by (in fact the dictionary uses the word *creative* in all the definitions it provides). One reason for that problem is that the word *creativity* is used interchangeably with other great words such as *imagination, ingenuity, innovation, intuition, invention, discovery*, and *originality*—all wonderful ideas for our students to strive toward.

A Thinking Question focus on thinking creatively drives us toward iden-tifying the facets that make up "Creative" thinking and include:

1. Combining pieces that have not been combined before,
2. Imagining and presenting things from new perspectives,
3. Focusing on new ways, new options, new modifications, and new connections to other concepts, and
4. Deferring judgment!! That means to first play and generate lots of ideas and *later* decide which idea is best (it is virtually impossible to do the two distinct thinking tasks—play versus pick—at the same time).

Diagram Explanation: Creativity is shown in the diagram as the infinity symbol for a reason. The diagram represents thinking of multiple concepts (not just the two shown), thinking of those pieces, thinking about the best pieces and then putting ideas from those concepts together in novel or unique or new ways. The more diverse the conceptual understandings, the more likely it is to create a new idea.

We need to generate lots (and lots) of ideas if we are to find the truly unique, novel, workable ideas that have a creative bent. Research in creativity points to the idea that only two or three ideas out of 100 fit that definition, and those ideas almost always occur toward the end of the list.

That means we need to think about our experiences, think about what we think we know about the concept, find the pieces, appraise those pieces, figure out what is the essence of the concept, re-consider our experiences in light of criteria to evaluate the concept—*and then* (doing that with many of our experiences) put pieces together in ways that have not been combined before!

Creativity Thinking Question Cue Words:

Ideas	Options
Ways	Changes
Changes	Opportunities
Possibilities	How else . . .
Improvements	New

List—followed by a number (75) may also be a creative cue word—if the task is to generate new ideas rather than list what is already known.

Creativity as a Thinking Question focuses on the creation of a Content-Specific Task. It is the extension of the concept you were trying to get them to understand (Induction) and how your field (science, language arts, math, etc.) goes about creating something new, showing something from a new perspective, or finding a new take on an old idea.

Content-Specific Tasks:

Build	Compose	
Act	Draw	Role Play
Experiment	Script	
Design	Tell	

Some examples: in science—a new experiment; in language arts—an original poem or short story; in history—a new biography; in PE—a new game; in music—a new composition or arrangement. Creativity says to students, "Create something new using the ideas we have already learned."

Creativity as Thinking Question is relevant to students because it allows them to put "their take" on the concept at hand, and to have valued the connections they see (and many others may not). Creativity extends their prior knowledge (the other Thinking Questions) into the future and creates a new and different reality.

Creativity is also Fun ("fun" being defined as "appropriately challenging"). Since there are many ways to be "right," pressures come not from being right or wrong but from making connections and being in fact "creative." The "right answer" is not the focal point; how you are perceiving the concept in new and different ways is.

While not textbook driven, creativity as Thinking Question is still very content heavy. To combine pieces not combined before means you must first know the pieces themselves. To put old ideas into a new context means you still must know the old idea and the new context. To create a new solution, you must first understand the problem and have researched current solutions. Creativity is all about using content as a tool to move learning forward.

In terms of thinking itself, creativity is grounded on all the other thinking skills (which have already been taught explicitly), so they begin the task knowing a lot (high chance for success, which is the greatest motivator). Risk of failure is small, thinking "outside the box" is valued and diversity is a benefit to creating original ideas and perspectives.

Since many students see the task itself as relevant, that means they also interact with the content more (time, effort, resources), which deepens their content knowledge and connections (a positive spiral).

Brainstorming rules are the foundation for many other creativity strategies: 1) No criticism is allowed; 2) the focus is on quantity; 3) the wilder the idea is the better; and 4) hitchhiking is OK (Davis, 2004). The tough part when being creative is to *not* judge ideas as they are said/written. Your "bad" idea might be the one idea that sparks an amazing idea in someone else. When brainstorming, perseverance is key—people must develop the disposition (and confidence) that they can in fact come up with many ideas or solutions.

Diversity of personal experiences is also a strength when being creative because people who are very different than you probably also have access to different life experiences, concepts and definitions than you do. That means that your group combinations can be more unique, more original and more workable! It pays to be creative with a diverse group (really).

It is becoming more and more obvious that the answers we grew up with in our industrialized society are not necessarily going to be the answers in tomorrow's world. Creativity is *not* a unitary ability, but is rather made up of a number of abilities: sensitivity to problems, fluency, flexibility, originality, elaboration and redefinition (Torrance, 1979). Everyone can increase their creativity when viewed with this perspective.

Teaching creativity requires that the teacher understand that opposition does exist to creativity. There are emotional roadblocks—fear of new ideas, the loss of comfort in knowing the one right answer and even the sense of belonging to people who think the same way you do. Cultural blocks, like social influence, expectations and conformity, also play a major role in stifling creativity, especially in schools.

Finally, mental blocks exist: habits, jumping to conclusions rather than looking for alternatives, and the opposition between creative changes and stabilizing forces. Also, the emphasis in schools themselves on recall, and the reproduction of a particular pattern of thinking or behavior, all combine to make the teaching of creativity an interesting experience.

For most school work, teachers can hope for originality but that isn't really the point of Creativity as a Thinking Question. The point of thinking creatively is the personalization of learning (and content understanding). Using information (what you think you know in theory) as a jumping-off point for further learning allows each learner the opportunity to *wallow* in the content as they try to figure something out (creativity is messy). They search for new ways and new perspectives, grapple with definitions and make connections to prior thoughts, beliefs and actions.

Finally, people who rate themselves as "highly creative" are also ranked high on self-actualization scale. If we want to grow our students into self-actualized participants in a democratic society, helping them learn to be more creative just seems to make sense (to us).

Classroom Examples:

1. List 50 ways to test the effectiveness of a fruit.
2. In what ways might we modify this story line for a new setting?
3. What ideas do you have for designing a conflict so that war would be inevitable after five years?
4. List 100 ideas for a new song title.

Rachel has participated fully in her group's brainstorming task. As the list is completed she asks, "Mr. James, we have about 25 really good ideas for our role play. We want to use them all but we obviously can't. Which idea should we pick?"

17

CRITICAL THINKING

The brainstorming is winding down, and Mr. James says, "OK, great work, everyone. Rachel tells me that you've got a bunch of workable ideas. Now let's pick some criteria by which to judge the value and likelihood of success for these ideas."

Critical Thinking as Thinking Question is the judging portion of Creativity. First, you think of lots of ideas, ways of thinking about something (creativity); then you use criteria (expert level is best) to pick your number one idea, which you will then DO (action)!

Critical Thinking requires:

1. Decision making (judging ideas),
2. Prediction of present situation into the future (guessing),
3. Consideration of consequences (creative/analysis task), and
4. A clear end-in-mind (the goal/vision or purpose).

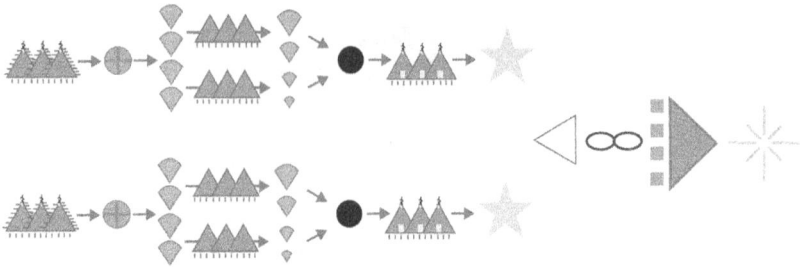

Diagram Explanation: You have been creative and generated a huge list of ideas (the infinity symbol). Now you have to pick your best idea. Critical Thinking here means to use expert-level criteria (the boxes) to pick your very best idea (the starburst). If the criteria change, so will the choice you make.

Critical Thinking Thinking Question Cue Words:

Predict	Forecast
Anticipate	What would happen if . . .
Hypothesize	What would be your number one . . .
Pick	Select
Select your best idea based upon	
X criteria	
Use the Idea Evaluator to pick	
your best option (appendix C)	

Critical thinking as a Thinking Question is really a two-part skill:

1. Identifying the criteria for the task at hand (the boxes in the diagram), and
2. Using those criteria to make your choice.

That means there are two key ideas when thinking Critically: 1) helping students experience the process of discovering expert-level criteria; and 2) using those criteria to pick something they will then DO. Both skills are fundamental to thinking critically—and complex to accomplish.

Experts in any field know what matters and that means the criteria by which choices are made (for that specific decision). An expert (frequently without thinking) looks at something and makes a decision about its quality.

Which product or idea is "best"? They consider multiple criteria and put those ideas together to decide what to actually do.

"Expertness" comes from: lots of prior experiences, lots of reflection about those experiences (analysis and appraisal), decisions made (or not made) and their consequences, and the rigorous study of the field. Experts do in fact "know" stuff. They have evaluations based upon field-appropriate criteria rather than opinions.

Any major type of decision requires the use of multiple criteria. Buying a house? Think location, size, schools nearby, space, neighbors, plumbing, electricity ... *Wow*—a realtor needs to consider many criteria. Same for buying a car (or van or truck, etc.). In fact, for most things we intend to purchase we almost always use many criteria (all very quickly and mostly implicitly).

The problem is when we attempt to "teach" critical thinking, we need to make those invisible criteria Explicit for our students. How can we hope to help them "think like an expert" if they do not know how an expert thinks (what they consider)?

Not only do they not know the criteria an expert uses, but they also do not know how they use them to make a final choice. This idea of identifying expert criteria and then using them to make a choice is a life-changing skill for our students.

People tell/expect students to be: thoughtful and rational, show good judgment, and pick wisely, but don't teach them *how* to do those tasks. It's as if adults assume students intentionally make bad choices. No—they did the best they could using the criteria and decision-making skills they had at that time.

Frequently our students do not consider:

1. Options/alternatives that exist (the creativity portion of any situation),
2. The criteria that connect your choice to your overall goal, and
3. Criteria that an expert would use.

Thinking like an expert (in terms of decision making) is complex when you do not have lots and lots of experiences, and even harder if you have never thought about what determines the quality of the thing in question. It is even hard for us who have multiple experiences with something—but we see those experiences from a different perspective.

Living in a house does not truly prepare you to be an expert house "buyer" (just like being a student does not prepare you for being a teacher!) A change in perspective matters—it requires a total "Re-think" of your experiences (and lots of focused learning experiences as well).

What can help is talking with experts and finding out what criteria they consider and how they use them together to make a decision. The difference between advice and information is advice tells you what you should do (the decision you should make), and information says that experts consider these ideas, information or criteria when making that kind of decision.

Criteria for any decision is complicated because they're so context specific. That means that a major change to the context changes how the criteria are applied. For example, one criteria that many of us may use when buying a car would be money. Change how much money you can spend and you fundamentally change the context (and maybe/probably the decision you make).

That means that what might be the "right" criteria at one time may not be right at another time; the context has changed. Understanding your criteria gives you a chance to think into the future—what would you choose with different criteria?

Ultimately, using Critical Thinking as a TQ is a prediction tool. When selecting anything you are predicting the best choice for yourself (it will best meet your needs at that time and place). You are saying that out of all the ideas you have created, using these criteria as most important, this one thing will best meet your needs.

Prediction based upon "thinking" is complex and contextual. It is not focused on The One Right Answer; it is focused on developing the thinking pattern that leads to a rationale for the decision.

People who think critically, when asked why they made that specific choice, answer, "I considered X, Y and Z," and then explain how they "considered those ideas (the pros and cons of each)," and finally used that thinking to select their number one idea. They have a "rationale" for the decision they made!

Classroom Examples:

1. Using these five criteria, pick your number one idea.
2. Pick four criteria and get them approved by me. Use them to select your best idea/option.

3. What criteria might someone else use? How would that influence their choice?
4. Predict the consequences of this choice.

Critical Thinking as a Future-Oriented Thinking Question requires that the teacher share expert criteria with their students. Having them pick their story topic? Tell them the criteria by which it will be assessed/evaluated. Having them pick their own experiment design? Tell them the criteria by which it will be assessed/evaluated. Having them pick their own new game? Tell them the criteria by which it will be assessed/evaluated. Give them the tools by which decisions are made.

Sarah says to the group, "I really like our best idea! It is unique, meets our needs, and has Mr. James' stamp of approval."

Ramone: "I really liked our second choice, but it would be way too long. Let's put it in our back pocket and see if we can't use it for something else."

Jack: "Sounds good to me. What's next?"

18

ACTION—PLAN AND DO (LIKE AN EXPERT)

Mr. James: "For the rest of the day, your task is to begin putting together a script or action plan for your Meeting-of-the Minds Role Play. After I approve your Civil War event and scenario, the next task will be to actually follow your plan and present and video record your Role Play for the class. Next Wednesday evening we will have an open house and invite your families and other people in to view what you've come up with."

Action in the school setting needs to be grounded in thinking rather than just doing. Time pressures, content exams, and school curriculums all point to the need to "cover" certain content. What if we could have students *act like experts* in the field—and make sure those actions are grounded in appropriate content?

Acting like an expert in any field includes: specific facts and knowledge, special skills directly related to what an expert actually does every day, and those dispositions that an expert would actually demonstrate on a daily basis. To DO something like an expert means to constantly Re-think, Re-visualize and Re-conceptualize what they think they know, can do and believe, using information as needed.

By using action as the culminating Thinking Question, you do not sacrifice content—you increase it. Students remember (long-term) content they have used.

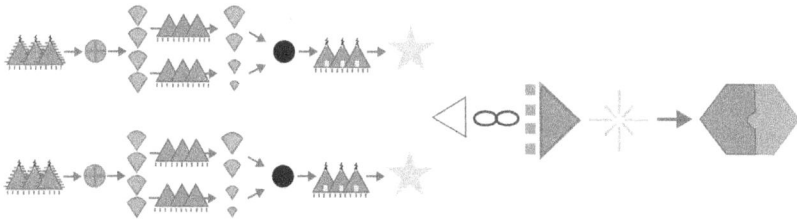

Diagram Explanation: Action—Plan and Do is the culmination of the Thinking Questions (for this one learning cycle). By this point students will have: multiple concrete experiences (the triangles) with the concept focal point (the circle), have analyzed (pie pieces), appraised (different size pie pieces), summarized (the small circle), and evaluated the pieces and important ideas (the star). They will also have thought about new ways of thinking and doing things (infinity) and then picked their very best idea (starburst) to Plan and Implement (hexagon puzzle piece). Their Plan and Implementation must be grounded in how the field goes about doing what they will be DOing!

Action Thinking Question Cue Words:

Plan	Outline
Steps	Web
Sequence	Write
Followed by	"Do it now!"

Action helps the individual translate theory into practice, and that is an important bridge to create. It is always easy to think, "I can do that," or "I could do that if I wanted to," yet experts in any field make the challenging appear easy. Experts have practiced their craft over and over again, sought new information, and used each experience to create new and deeper understandings. They constantly Re-view, Re-vise and Re-think what they currently do, know and believe.

Experts take their number one idea (using appropriate/expert criteria), plan their next task or performance, and DO it for real (not just in their heads). They might: write the script for their number one idea—then perform it; design their number one experiment—then conduct it; or create their number one new game—then play it. And even as they are DOing it, they are already considering ways to make it better (a continual Re-think mentality).

For our students (and all those curricular expectations), action also needs to be directly aligned with the original concept development idea. Knowledge (facts), skills, and dispositions must be experienced, explained, and assessed so that students may act in ways that extend their thinking, build new skills and their deepest beliefs.

Action (grounded in experiences and information) requires a two-step thinking process: (1) Planning and (2) Doing.

1. Planning includes the WWWWWH (Who, What, When, Where, Why, and How) features of any task. It includes the: materials, time estimates, resources that will be needed (and obtained), the process (steps) that will be followed, task or job allocations, communication strategies, checkpoints, evaluations and assessments, and the alignment of the task to the final assessment criteria.

And

2. Doing the plan! This step of course requires constant Re-visions and adjustments toward the assessment criteria. Plans are not the reality of the thing. Constant checkpoints, the gathering of more information, modifications of the plan, and cutting and pasting are all normal features of any DOing task.

DOing makes theory come alive. Sounds easy to use Civil War methods to bake some bread? Now grind it—by hand—find some yeast, build the fire, then bake the bread. Want to get a paper published? Find the magazine, follow their steps, submit the written paper, then wait (up to six weeks).

DOing things is fun and challenging (and that's a good thing). We value (an emotion) things that we have struggled to accomplish. Overcoming the struggles makes the learning journey worthwhile. The enactment of the plan is a major part of the journey.

One other thing about plans: They almost never turn out the way we anticipate! Plans are our "first best guess" about how things will go. In reality (DOing the plan) we almost always have to Re-think, Re-plan, and Re-organize. Yet, having a plan is crucial to success (as long as we see the plan as a work-in-progress).

One of the beauties about DOing is that the end product is worth sharing—with other classes, parents/guardians, other teachers, board members and community members. It says, "This is what I have created!" Action allows for a concrete product and proves to the self what has been learned. "I did this," and "I learned this!"

Student actions demonstrate the depth of their conceptual knowledge of the concept you had them experience at the beginning. Their actions integrate the knowledge, skills and dispositions (back to part I) you were hoping to help them learn. Action as part of Thinking Questions is:

Content heavy (facts and connections),
Skill heavy (repetition and practice), and
Disposition heavy (think like an expert in the field).

Finally, action also completes the learning cycle! The entire Thinking Question sequence started with concrete experiences—and ends with concrete experiences (at a more sophisticated level). Students now know more, can do more and are more aware of the dispositions that reflect their deepest beliefs. When taught Explicitly and Intentionally, the Thinking Question sequence helps them build their self-confidence and moves them toward self-awareness.

Classroom Examples:

1. Compose your number one poem and present it to the school during our annual Poetry Slam.
2. Now plan and create your own authentic wax museum for presentation in two weeks.
3. Write the rules for your new game, which your parents will play at our next open house.
4. Plan and Conduct your own experiment and then write it up for binding and presentation in the school library.

Eventually, the students settle on a plan. Mr. James approves their Civil War event—a small battle in the South that causes a family to lose their home and barn. They write their script for the aftermath of the event. Ramone plays the farmer's son, Jack the Captain whose force caused the buildings to burn, Sarah the girlfriend of the soldier who lit the house on fire, and Rachel the widowed mother of the farmer.

They each get very excited about their role play, for very different reasons: Sarah has always wanted to try her hand at writing and directing a script; Jack—this is what he lives for; Ramone—he gets to shift from a supporting role on the football team to being the key figure in the role play; and Rachel—playing a mother figure gives her a chance to imagine what her mother might actually be thinking. They are each committed to their own learning.

All knowledge is personal knowledge—and is not the same thing as the accumulation of information (factoids). Personal knowledge is the interaction between information and the human experience. I get to choose what I believe, the skills I learn, and the information that I think matters most (to me, at that time and at that place).

DOing something that is grounded in what an expert might do requires that I "think like an expert." Most experts produce things that have an external audience. Experts demonstrate their learning to a knowledgeable audience (even if it's just other experts in the field), which has its own type(s) of pressure. Performances are exciting (and scary and nerve wracking and worthwhile and fun!).

DOing something with a concept that students have experienced, studied, summarized, compared, and ranked allows them to create their own "knowledge" about that concept. They have been the ones to do the thinking—Re-visiting their own experiences as well as new information.

Last night Mr. James' class had an open house and parents, guardians, and other family members came and watched class members on video recordings act out their Meeting-of-the-Mind Role Plays. Almost all the students were excited to showcase their learning and most everyone left feeling proud of their accomplishments.

It was fun for Mr. James to see the students interact with the adults who could make the event, and he gave students whose parents/guardians could not attend the YouTube link and a CD so they could share at home. School administrators were impressed by both the video recordings and how many parents and guardians came to watch.

Today Mr. James chats with the class. He begins by asking a few questions:

1. So, what have we learned about perspectives and historical events?
2. Why is the Civil War such an important event in US history?
3. How does what we have learned this unit change how we think about each other?
4. What are some things you have learned about yourself?

As Mr. James listens to their answers and commentary, he compares their answers to HIS ends-in-mind for the unit:

1. Knowledge: Have they learned the facts about the Civil War he set out for them? How well have they connected those facts into personal knowledge?
2. Skills: Have they learned how to triangulate information, find and take the source into account, see multiple perspectives about any event, distinguish between fact and fiction, and see things without 20/20 hindsight?
3. Dispositions: Have they learned how to think like "historians," create action plans and follow them through, look for multiple right answers, and come to own their own learning?

Mr. James teaches people (rather than history). He takes them from where they are and moves them over on their own personal learning (and life) journey. He has come to love the fact that they talk like historians, can find primary sources and play with multiple views of reality.

Ultimately, Mr. James loves how he has made himself dispensable—his students have learned how to learn without him (at least for this learning cycle)!

V

MAKING ART

Art may be defined (*Merriam-Webster*, 2002) as the "conscious use of skill and creative imagination in the production of aesthetic objects." While our students may not exactly be "aesthetic objects," providing learning opportunities that help them learn how to think certainly requires skill and creative imagination.

Planning for student thinking is different than hoping for or recognizing thinking when you see or hear it. Planning for thinking requires both the knowledge and the skills of: each of the individual pieces, sequencing things so they cumulatively build upon each other, Re-mediating flaws in student thinking, and beginning the entire enterprise with an explicit end-in-mind.

Teaching others to think is an art. Every class is different and every day our audience changes. Some students learn in ways that we can appreciate; others need a more nuanced approach. Some students have life issues; others come to school ready to learn. Our jobs are all about being *artful*—on a daily basis!

To make good art consistently requires the knowledge and the skills and the dispositions to embrace those changing contexts that are our audience.

19

PLANNING FOR THINKING QUESTIONS

Mr. James' students love his enthusiasm and high energy, parents like him because he knows their kids, and the administration values his work ethic and kindness. His students regularly pass the AP exams with high scores, and regularly ask challenging questions.

His teaching colleagues know he cares about his students and his content, and so while they do not understand why or how he teaches the way he does, they like and value him as a colleague.

Creating connected experiences for students with an explicit end-in-mind is art. It is a dynamic process, which means that it is always in flux, always changing and morphing into something else. One experience, one comment, one new insight can change the entire process (and product)—and that's OK—and a fun way to teach!

Mr. James has been teaching his thinking-focused Civil War unit for a couple of years. Rachel, Jack, Ramone, and Sarah get to experience the unit after Mr. James has been able to tinker, experiment, and Re-structure the unit a couple of times. He regularly makes changes according to student feedback, which he collects at the end of each semester.

This year, Ramone asked about doing a Q-and-A session after the Meeting of the Minds showing—he was particularly proud of his group's work and would've loved an opportunity to talk more about why they made the choices they did and to explain some of the more intricate parts of the piece. It's an interesting idea, and Mr. James takes it into account for next year.

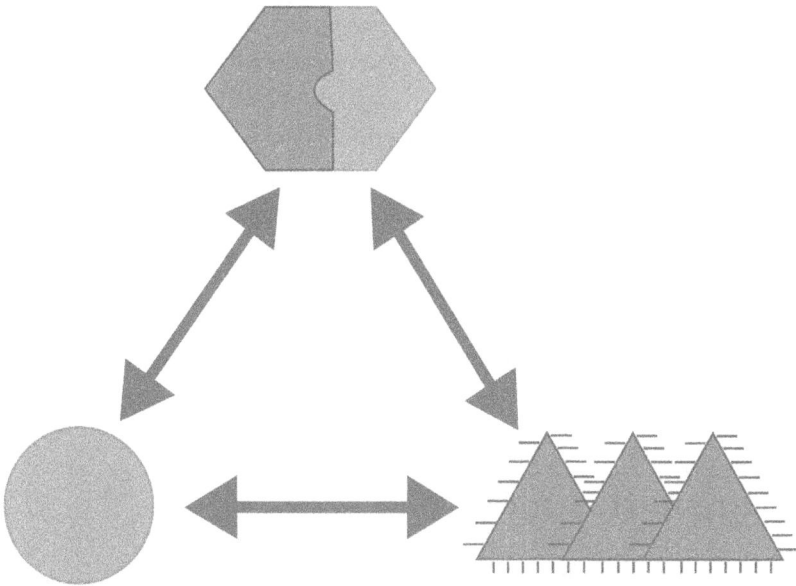

Diagram Explanation: Notice that all the arrows are double arrows—that means each idea works with the other ideas, and when they work together they influence each other. The three key components for planning include: 1) Action—Plan and Do, 2) Concept Identification, and 3) Experience Choices.

Many teachers, including Mr. James, were never taught to teach thinking. They have to find it, to discover it for themselves. For Mr. James, it might have happened like this, three years ago:

Mr. James was reading "The Three Little Pigs" to his children (which they love) when his wife brought in a copy of "The True Story of the Three Little Pigs." He read the story to his kids and they had a very interesting conversation about "being a wolf" and how the same story can have different points of view. Later that night (or early the next morning—he had a tough time going to sleep that night) Mr. James had an a-ha moment.

His thinking process looked something like this:

If "The Three Little Pigs" has more than one perspective, wouldn't that be true for one of his favorite topics (the Civil War)?

And wouldn't teaching about different perspectives of the same event be more interesting than teaching the same Civil War facts semester after semester?

And wouldn't personalizing history make the content more relevant to his students?

And what did he want his students to really learn about history—especially with all the technology they have access to?

With these questions in mind, Mr. James began to plan for a brand new unit—a version of which he would teach to Ramone, Jack, Sarah, and Rachel a couple of years later.

1. ACTION—PLAN AND DO

Backwards Design (Wiggins and McTighe, 1998) emphasizes knowing what you want students to have learned at the end of the unit before you start any other planning. That means you know what Final Tasks the students will be working toward *and* how you will Assess those tasks before you begin any other planning. Beginning with the end-in-mind also means to consider both Content *and* making learning Relevant for your students.

Final Tasks

The Final Tasks for any unit of instruction need to be worthy of sharing with an external audience, allow students to personalize content facts and allow for creative ways of thinking about their learning (new perspectives, new connections and new insights).

When the Task at hand is interesting to students they give of their time, efforts and resources. They are said to be "motivated" because they are engaged in their own learning.

Mr. James thinks about his storytelling skills with the Three Little Pigs. His kids love his voices, his verbals and nonverbals, and love to participate in his storytelling. He decides to have his students become storytellers of different perspectives—about people who experienced the Civil War from different perspectives; blacks, whites, Northerners, Southerners, mothers, fathers, old, young, rich, poor, educated, and not formally educated.

He also decides to have them write their histories and put them together into a text for others. Mr. James decides that doing "papers" only for the teacher does not allow students to share their learning with their parents—and certainly not with the community. Not only that, but knowing your piece will be published and displayed for others to see adds some pressure to doing a good job ☺!

Finally, he decides to invite parents and community members into his class and watch students interact with each other as they role play the people they have written their stories about. He plans to video record these "Meeting of the Mind" dialogues and invite parents to watch their children perform their roles. He will ask his students to showcase their learning to the people who care most about them—what could be more relevant than that?

Deciding upon the Final Task allows the teacher to make coherent curricular and learning decisions with those Final Tasks in mind. This content—In (needed for the Final Task). This content—Out (interesting but not helpful to the Final Task). This Learning Activity—In (makes explicit a required Knowledge, Skill or Disposition). This Learning Activity—Out (Fun but not crucial at this time).

Focusing on the Final Task allows the teacher to make instructional choices that are both Explicit and Intentional.

Assessments: Assessments and Evaluations tell everyone where to focus their efforts, that these Facts, these Skills and these Dispositions matter. They matter so much they will assessed and evaluated both during and at the end of the unit.

Knowledge: Mr. James knows the importance of the AP exam to students, parents and the administration. He also realizes that there is more to history than the accumulation of facts (from one perspective).

He plans to create a list of the most important facts from the AP exam and content standards and tell the students right up front what those are. He then plans to have them use those facts in their perspective stories. He will also give a content exam at the end of the unit to make sure they know those facts.

Skills: Writing a "history" of an event from a person's perspective will allow him to teach "historical writing" skills. Triangulation, primary sources, format, voice and context are all important features of historical writings. He will expect them to provide context for their person, an individual perspective of an event he will choose, and to write with that framework rather than the 20/20 hindsight version of their current perspectives.

Dispositions: Mr. James also wants his students to develop their "history dispositions." He wants to allow them to see that there are multiple right perspectives of any event and that studying history does not mean to always judge historical figures. Context matters—and the development of empathy rests upon the foundation of seeing things from another person's point of view.

Finally Mr. James plans to talk with his students after all the assessments are complete. He wants to "debrief" their experiences (from all their perspectives) so they can create a shared knowledge about what their learning journey entailed. He knows that each product is in fact its own experience (a triangle) and they are then able to start a new learning journey with an experience that has shaped their thinking.

2. CONCEPT IDENTIFICATION

For content issues, backwards design includes looking over your school curriculum (if you have one and actually know where it is!), the AP exam itself (or at least the notes they let you see), and local, state, and national standards. Everyone it seems wants to tell you what content to teach, and every year it seems the list gets longer and longer.

Fortunately, in every content area there are some ideas that hold the field together. Those ideas are called things like: Central Concepts, Themes, Big Ideas, Threads, Strands, etc. What they all refer to are those simple, Big (enduring) ideas that cut across all the disciplines within one field (appendix D).

For example, in science one Big Idea is that of energy. That means when scientists talk about cellular respiration (energy) in biology, they can also connect that idea to reactions in chemistry (energy) and plate tectonics in geology (energy). The Big Ideas allow teachers to "connect" concepts (the circle in the diagrams) from one discipline to another, and help students realize that what they have already learned is still useful and important. Prior learning acts as the foundation for future learning, in whatever discipline!

Note 1: All the details (facts) that everyone wants students to "know" really just illuminate and add detail to the central concepts of the field.

Note 2: Since the Big Ideas in any field (i.e., energy in science) cut across all the disciplines (biology, chemistry, etc.), the teacher has the option to emphasize any central concept for any specific content. For example, a teacher could use the Civil War to teach about people (our example) or resources, or power, or time, etc. What the teacher ultimately assesses tells everyone which Big Idea they are working on at this point in time.

Mr. James decides that the concept he will focus on for his unit will be People (a Social Studies Central Concept). Not just people in general but how each individual has their own Perspective about any event that takes place. He believes he can connect those ideas to helping his students develop their ability to be empathetic—a relevant topic for many of his students trying to understand their peers.

Content Choice

Every teacher is required by their school to teach specific content, and most teachers like the content anyway. Content is in fact important because thinking requires something to think about.

Mr. James has decided to focus on the Civil War as his content platform. It is a section on the AP exam, all the standards mention it, and besides that he is a Civil War buff and knows some parents and community groups that do Civil War reenactments.

He believes that he can use that event to "teach" the Big Idea of "People." Thinking about the Three Little Pigs, he wants to help his students realize there are many different Perspectives to any single event.

He also decides that what he really wants to have his students learn is how to think "like a historian." He wants to help them put together a "history thinking template" for studying different events in time. He believes that helping them learn to "think like a historian" will be an investment of time rather than a cost. They will be able to use their "history thinking template" over and over again—knowing what counts (to historians).

Relevance and Content

Creating lessons that make learning "relevant" requires understanding what needs (Maslow's Hierarchy of Needs) your students have right now, today. It means *using* content as the vehicle to teach students something important, something that will "enhance their Quality of Life" right now—not some far-off day in the future.

Fortunately, DOing what experts in any field actually do is pretty interesting. Writing/Creating plays, finding a pattern that explains a set of phenomena, finding an answer to a question you have, or creating a workout that works for you—things that experts DO also seem to meet people's needs.

The interesting thing about DOing what experts do is that those actions are grounded in facts (knowledge) and skills. In other words you need to know some stuff (content) to DO what they do (skills). Want to fish? Better know some stuff about fish, and fishing gear and strategies. Want to write a play? Better know some stuff about the concept for the play and how to structure your writing. Want to illuminate a pattern of events? Better know about representations and operations.

The beauty of DOing activities is that the content you learn makes sense to you. You *need* to know those facts to accomplish your task, not just because someone told you to memorize those factoids. We all know lots and lots of facts about things we love to do—in fact sometimes it is scary how much "trivia" we know about our hobbies and interests.

3. EXPERIENCE CHOICES

Once you as teacher have developed a good sense of what you want for your students at the end of the unit, your teaching dilemma becomes "What concrete, three-dimensional experiences do I need to provide so that their thinking (concept development) is grounded in personal experiences rather than information filtered by many others?"

The most challenging realization is that those concrete experiences you provide will be the basis for *all* the other thinking questions you will ask—from induction to creativity. The student's final project will ultimately be the extension of thought from those very basic, very foundational personal experiences.

Going back to the Experiences diagram, it is important to realize those experiences (plural) need to include their senses, access their different ways of processing that input, and have an emotional component to make it memorable, all while helping make their mental models (of thought) explicit to them.

So Mr. James decides to start the unit with the following six experiences:

1. Diaries and letters from a wide variety of people involved in the Civil War as well as audiotapes of slaves from that time period.
2. Newspapers, magazines, and ads from that time period.
3. Food and drinks from that time period (they will have to use a Civil War recipe and make something to share in class).
4. A medical kit, glasses, and sickness remedies from that time period (as well as death and wounded statistics).
5. Song lyrics, musical instruments, and a Civil War dance.
6. Clothes, transportation devices, and delivery schedules. Everyone has to wear a period costume during class (thanks to the reenactment group and the theatre department).

Good thinking requires powerful experiences and information to think about! Those powerful concrete experiences become the "memory hook" that ties information together and allows students to *make* their own knowledge.

FINAL NOTE: EXPERIENCES AND ACTION

We are all functions of our life experiences (with a genetic twist). Having a powerful life experience fundamentally changes who you are. The key to creating the "Art" of teaching thinking is connecting the experiences you provide, plus the ones they already have toward your end-in-mind for their learning.

The Art of teaching thinking means the experiences you provide have to 1) be robust enough; 2) be diverse enough; and 3) set students up for success at the end (write a history and role play their person from history). Will those experiences you have provided allow for a deep and complex conversation about "perspectives"? Will those experiences be so diverse that easy answers will be hard to find? Will there be enough commonality so that the concept of Perspective and People becomes their frame of reference?

Those thoughts, decisions, and planning will determine the quality of their historical writings and their ability to role play their person with honesty and thoughtfulness.

20

CREATING ART WITH THINKING QUESTIONS

Doing anything well requires that the individual: knows some stuff (facts and how those facts are connected); does some stuff (skills and techniques); and wants to do it (spend their Time, Effort and Resources on the task at hand—Dispositions). At the highest level of anything, experts in that area have committed themselves to "learning" those things.

Artists in any field know what matters most. They know the field-specific knowledge and the skills and act with content-specific dispositions. They know how the small, seemingly insignificant things work together to make their product "beautiful." The things they create are beautiful in their apparent simplicity—they make the incredibly complex look simple.

Teaching people to think is an art. We work with people who change from day to day and sometimes moment to moment. We are mostly unaware of how they see (and smell and hear) the world, how they process those experiences, what mental models they hold and what range of emotions influence their lives. What fun!!

A teacher's beautiful artwork, our product, are the individuals who leave our classrooms. We need to know their strengths and weaknesses, realize that they are doing the best they can, see diversity as a strength in almost any endeavor, and help them live their lives with an action-orientation. Teacher artists help create individuals who own their own lives.

Creating opportunities for students to learn how to think Explicitly and Intentionally is the work of a teacher artist. It is all about connections (between the different ways of thinking), scaffolding those thoughts and ideas to further understanding, and connecting those thoughts to powerful end-in-minds. Here our end-in-mind is to make ourselves dispensable!

Teaching thinking is about empowering our students to create their own future (not to reproduce the past). They need to be aware of their own experiences, see their own mental models, think for themselves and live with an action-orientation.

The intent of the diagrams in this book is to make Explicit the complexity of thinking. Memorization is easy—either you have memorized the facts or you haven't. Thinking requires a constant Re-visiting of what you think you know—in light of new experiences, information or perspectives of past experiences. Thinking is hard intellectual work (hard—yet interesting).

Providing thinking diagrams empowers the learner to make explicit their own thoughts and why they think the way they do: "Because of this experience I think like this," "This new experience might cause me to Re-think my conceptual understanding," or "Creating a new experiment makes that information pretty important to me."

Finally, the series of Thinking Questions realistically represents a "learning cycle" across time. We start with 3-D concrete experiences—and then while DOing something with that concept we create new concrete experiences—which very well might change how we think, what we can do and maybe even what we believe. We begin the next learning task from a very different place than where we started!

A

ANSWERS TO THE ANALYSIS QUESTIONS

1. List the parts of a fruit.

   Students would have to have experienced a variety of the following:

Apple	Pear
Orange	Strawberry
Pepper	Cucumber
Okra	Pecan
Hazelnut	Zucchini

2. Create a story map for journeys.

   Students would have to have experienced a variety of the following:

   1. Elizabeth Gilbert's *Eat Pray Love*
   2. Cheryl Strayed's *Wild*
   3. Jack Kerouac's *On the Road*
   4. Mark Twain's *The Adventures of Huckleberry Finn*
   5. Che Guevara's *The Motorcycle Diaries*

3. What commonalities are there between people identified as "explorers"?

   Students would have to have experienced a variety of the following:

   1. Amelia Earhart
   2. Sacajawea
   3. Henry Morton Stanley
   4. Marco Polo
   5. Gertrude Bell

4. What do these "invasion games" have in common?

Students would have to have experienced a variety of the following:

1. Basketball
2. Soccer
3. Football
4. Capture the flag
5. Hockey

B

MEETING
OF THE MINDS

This idea is a modification of a TV show named *Meeting of Minds with Steve Allen*. Allen clarified at the time,

> The idea is that every syllable will be part of an actual quotation. The degree of the exact quotation varies from character to character. In the case of some people who played important roles in the drama of history, of course, there is no record of anything they ever said or wrote.
>
> Two examples that come to mind are Cleopatra and Attila the Hun. Nevertheless, they were both fascinating characters for our show. And there's nothing difficult in creating dialogue for them. You bring factual information into conversational form—and commit no offense in doing so.
>
> *Meeting of Minds* encourages the viewer and reader to become more familiar with the great thinkers and doers of the past and to whet their appetites for more research and study. It is an exciting classroom tool (through audiocassettes, videocassettes and books) for students of history and philosophy.
>
> I felt that putting the greatest figures of all time together and showing them interacting was an entertaining way not only to have a better understanding of what is going on in the world today, but also to be in a better position to make decisions for the future.

The idea presented here is that each student pick (or be assigned) a specific person from history. They research and study that person and then are asked to "role play" that person—asking and answering questions as if they were actually that historical figure.

Some examples:

Science—assign different students to be different parts of the cell—and then have them converse about getting some task accomplished.

Math—assign different students to be different functions—and then to rank order their importance.

English—assign different students to be different parts of speech—and then have them talk about how they interact with each other.

Assigning specific prompts before the role play allows students to focus their research and to extend their information gathering to questions that are relevant today.

Criteria for Assessment of Student Role Plays might be:

Understanding of the topic under discussion (the prompts you have assigned—content)

Ability to Accurately Portray their Role-Play Views

Presentation Participation (during the Role Play)

Costumes/Mannerisms/Props

C

IDEA EVALUATOR

CRITERIA

IDEAS								Total	Rank

HOW TO USE AN IDEA EVALUATOR

The "best" ideas go down the side—usually picked from your creative list.

Approved criteria for the decision (you will need to approve them) go in the slanted lines.

Criteria change for the decision that is being made!

Using one criteria at a time, give a value to the idea on a scale from 1 to 5 (5 being the highest score).

Use the same criteria to evaluate each idea (go down the column).

More than one of any number can be assigned to different ideas (more than one 5).

Do each criteria evaluating each idea.

Once all ideas have been evaluated by all the criteria, add each row (total score).

The number one idea is the one with the highest overall score.

Note: When students are asked to explain how they got their number one idea—and then explain how they assigned a criteria score for the idea—they are in all actuality giving you their "rationale" for the decision they have made (Explicitly).

D

CENTRAL CONCEPTS

Art

1. Production
2. Creativity
3. Literacy/Responding
4. Connecting

English/Language Arts

1. Rhetoric
2. Analysis
3. Inquiry
4. Communication/Expression

Foreign Language

1. Communication
2. Cultures
3. Comparisons
4. Connections
5. Communities

Math

1. Communication
2. Representations
3. Relationships
4. Operations

Music

1. Time (beat/pulse, meter, rhythm)
2. Pitch
3. Melody
4. Harmony
5. Text
6. Form
7. Expression (tempo, timbre, texture, dynamics, articulation)

PE/Health

1. Fitness concepts
2. Motor learning and development
3. Movement concepts
4. Skill themes
5. Biomechanics
6. Systems

Science

1. Classification
2. Cycles
3. Energy
4. Change/Balance
5. Systems

Social Studies

1. People (place, environment)
2. Time (continuity, change)
3. Power
4. Resources
5. Conflict
6. Exploration

REFERENCES

Armstrong, T. (1993). *7 Kinds of Smart*. New York: Penguin Books.

Davis, G. (2004). *Creativity Is Forever* (5th Edition). Dubuque, IA: Kendall/Hunt Publishing.

Dewey, J. (1934). *Experience and Education*. New York: Simon and Schuster.

Gardner, H. (1983). *Frames of Mind*. New York: BasicBooks.

Glasser, W. (1998). *Choice Theory*. New York: HarperCollins Publisher.

Kolis, M. (2011). *Student Relevance Matters*. New York: Rowman & Littlefield.

Kuhn, T. (1970). *The Structure of Scientific Revolutions*. Chicago: The University of Chicago Press.

Merriam-Webster's Collegiate Dictionary (10th Edition) (2002). Springfield, MA: Merriam-Webster, Inc.

Senge, P. (1990). *The Fifth Discipline*, New York: Currency and Doubleday.

Torrance, E. P. (1979). *The Search for Satori and Creativity*. Buffalo, NY: Creative Education Foundation, Inc.

Wiggins, G., and McTighe, J. (1998). *Understanding by Design*. Alexandria, VA: ASCD.

www.ingramcontent.com/pod-product-compliance
Lightning Source LLC
Chambersburg PA
CBHW030654270326
41929CB00007B/353